What does hospitality look like? This is [...] book *People Are the Mission* helps us! Da[...] want to feel respected, honored. They don[...] want shock and awe, and they don't want to be an afterthought. They just want to know you care, for real. If you're a leader in a church or business and you want to improve your culture of hospitality, then you'll love Danny's new book. It's a must-read!

DAN T. CATHY, Chairman and CEO of Chick-fil-A

When Danny leads, I follow him. When he writes, I read it. So should you.

JASON YOUNG, Director of Guest Services, North Point Ministries, Atlanta, GA

The gospel is like a song. It has both lyrics and a musical score. Those who water down the lyrics to make the song more palatable may gain a crowd. But they'll inevitably lose the gospel. In the same way, those who allow the gospel to be presented in a lame, unwelcoming, or culturally out-of-touch environment end up singing true words that nobody listens to. Danny Franks has written a helpful and balanced book that corrects the pendulum swing between these two extremes and connects the dots between staying true to the gospel message and adapting to the culture we live in. If you desire a guest-friendly, gospel-centric ministry, this is a book you need to read.

LARRY OSBORNE, pastor and author, North Coast Church

Writing from a heart captivated by the gospel, Danny Franks has delivered a powerful, impressive work that church leaders—regardless of position—will find tremendously helpful in establishing a culture of hospitality throughout their church and ministry areas.

People Are the Mission balances a keen intellectual understanding of the nuts and bolts of hospitality with a gospel-centered foundation. This compelling combination comes from Danny's practical, lived-out, and loved-through leadership with hundreds of leaders at his own church and across the country.

Using his razor-sharp wit, Danny makes his point, driving right to the heart of the matter with a balance of aw-shucks genuineness wrapped up in instantly applicable lessons you will immediately grasp. *People Are the Mission* will become one of your most-used and most often referred-to training helps for years to come. Pick up a copy today, start reading it tonight, and begin applying it tomorrow.

BOB ADAMS, Guest Experience Navigator, Auxano, Houston, TX

Evangelism and discipleship, two oars attached to one boat, are essential to carrying out the Great Commission. In *People Are the Mission*, Danny Franks shows us the importance of attracting people, without compromising the gospel message, to empower them for ministry. I am grateful for Danny's approach of helping move people from being consumers to commissioned partners in ministry.

ROBBY GALLATY, pastor, Long Hollow Baptist Church; author, *Growing Up* and *The Forgotten Jesus*

In *People Are the Mission*, my friend Danny moves beyond excellent technique with weekend crowds to the transformation of God's grace in an individual's journey. When Danny writes of truth, he does so with deep conviction. When he speaks of grace, he does so with personal compassion. And when he uses humor (and he does), watch out—you're either about to be knocked off balance by his sucker-punch challenge or he's giving you a chance to recover respectfully, because that spot right between your eyes still hurts. Danny's conviction, compassion, and challenge are motivated by his belief that people matter to God, and people will believe they do, when we make loving them our sole mission, or our "soul mission." For their sake and God's honor, read this book.

MARK WALTZ, author of *First Impressions: Creating Wow Experiences in Your Church*; trainer, LifePlan Coach, Because People Matter, LLC

PEOPLE
ARE THE
MISSION

How Churches Can Welcome **Guests**
Without Compromising the **Gospel**

DANNY FRANKS

ZONDERVAN

People Are the Mission
Copyright © 2018 by Danny Franks

This title is also available as a Zondervan ebook.

Requests for information should be addressed to:
Zondervan, *3900 Sparks Dr. SE, Grand Rapids, Michigan 49546*

Library of Congress Cataloging-in-Publication Data

Names: Franks, Danny (Pastor), author.
Title: People are the mission : how churches can welcome guests without compromising
    the gospel / Danny Franks.
Description: Grand Rapids, MI : Zondervan, [2018]
Identifiers: LCCN 2017046473 | ISBN 9780310538677 (softcover)
Subjects: LCSH: Church membership. | Choice of church.
Classification: LCC BV820 .F73 2018 | DDC 253--dc23 LC record available at
    https://lccn.loc.gov/2017046473

Cover design: Thinkpen Design
Interior design: Kait Lamphere

Printed in the United States of America

To Merriem (of course).
Thank you for encouraging me
to write this stuff down.

Contents

Foreword by J. D. Greear

Danny and I were both discipled by flannelgraph Jesus. Our first conceptions of the Son of God were formed by felt-backed images of a gentle Jesus holding kids, petting lambs, and guiding sinners with his serene face and calming eyes. One image we never saw on flannelgraph, however, was angry Jesus with a bullwhip.

Yet we find that Jesus in Scripture. And I know you are thinking this is a terrible introduction to a book on biblical hospitality, but the Gospels tell us that there were times Jesus got angry. Interestingly, the angriest we ever see him get is when he observes Jewish leaders cluttering up the Court of the Gentiles with the buying and selling of temple sacrifices. Not only was Jesus angry over the profiteering now encumbering God's free and gracious offer of salvation, he was angry over *where* they were running their racket: the outer court that God had established for Gentiles to observe and experience the gospel. With the backing of a whip, Jesus exclaimed, "My house was intended to be a house of prayer for all nations, but you have turned it into a den of thieves!"

Typically, we focus on only the last part of Jesus's rebuke and think that so long as we are not price-gouging items we sell in our lobbies we are safe from Jesus's whip. But the more important part of Jesus's rebuke is the last part, the "why" he was so angry at their profiteering: "My house was designated to be a house of prayer for the nations." Jesus was angry not only at what they were *doing*, but also at what they were *obscuring*. They had transformed the only open-access point for the Gentiles into a catalogue of comforts and conveniences for the already saved. They had transformed a portal for the outsider into a dumbwaiter for the insider.

Would Jesus not feel the same today about churches that fail to mind those portals where outsiders can observe the glories of the gospel in action? In churches today we "clutter up the Court of the Gentiles" when we fail to make accommodations for the outsider in our preaching, music, language, the practice of our traditions, our children's programs, and our parking and signage. By not thinking of the "observing outsiders," we create some of the same roadblocks for "Gentiles" as the Jews did in Jesus's day. How must Jesus feel when a church refuses even to *consider* what it needs to change to reach the community and the next generation? When they care more about their conveniences and comfort than they do the lost all around them?

Please don't misunderstand me. I don't mean that churches ought to turn to smoke and mirrors (or, in our case, laser light shows and subwoofers). We don't have a single moving light in our church. Sure, the world may be entertained by musical flair and entertaining programs, but they'll never be transformed by them. As the apostle Paul said, the power to transform sinners comes from the foolish message of Jesus crucified (1 Corinthians 2:2–4). That will always be at the core of what we, the church, are called to proclaim. But how can they encounter the gospel if we don't welcome them into a place where they can hear it?

At our church, Pastor Danny has taught us that the gospel is offensive, but nothing else should be. We make every effort to attract unbelievers to our services and make the gospel accessible to them. And we make no apology for it.

That's what excites me about this book. Perhaps more than anyone else at our church, Danny has led the way in creating an environment that reflects the gospel-disposition virtue of hospitality. We don't strive to excel in hospitality because it brings people back to our church, but because it best reflects how Christ treated us.

Pastor Danny has been with the Summit since the early days, and he has taught us that everything we do as a church *speaks*. The sermon, as he so often repeats, starts in the parking lot. Thus, the question is not *if* we're sending a message, only *what* message we are sending. Your guest services write the intro to the sermon. What kind of introduction are you giving?

In fact, that line I just used—"The gospel is offensive; nothing else should be"—I'm 99 percent sure I stole that from Danny.

The book you hold in your hands is not just theory from a guy who thinks he's witty (though he *does* think he's witty, and 82.6 percent of the jokes he attempts are indeed funny); it's a collection of the principles that I've seen in practice every single weekend at our church—principles that have been an enormous part of why we by God's grace have maintained a consistent growth curve for almost two decades.

Your church's preaching and worship styles may *draw* a crowd, but to *keep* a crowd, people must sense that you love them, that you expected them, and that you can't wait for them to return. Finally, here is a book that tells you *how to make that happen*.

The mission of God is to reach people, and the vehicle God has chosen to reach them is the church. Because the church belongs to God, not us, then we're always putting our preferences on hold in favor of his mission, doing whatever it takes to get the gospel to the lost. *People are the mission*, and if you want to know what that means for the guest services at your church, read on.

J. D. Greear, author and pastor of the
Summit Church, Raleigh-Durham, NC

Introduction: A Wee Little Man and a Tale of Two Churches

His sandals kicked up small clouds of dust as he made his way down the side street. The midday sun was unforgiving, but for the moment, the heat and his sweat didn't matter. He was a man on a mission with a deadline. As he walked—no, rushed—past each building, he glanced down alleys and around corners to determine his next move and thought to himself, "Not there. Not yet. Maybe the next left . . ."

The buzz in town had started earlier that morning. Jesus was coming to Jericho. *That* Jesus. Jesus-of-Nazareth Jesus. Jesus the revered, Jesus the reviled, Jesus the pot stirrer, Jesus the crowd gatherer, Jesus the miracle worker. The latest rumor was that he had healed a roadside beggar of his blindness. *Healed* him. The beggar had woken up like it was any other day—unable to distinguish day from night except for the heat of the Middle Eastern sun on his face—yet by that night he could see everything that had been unseen since his birth. And now this Jesus—Jesus the healer, Jesus the eye opener, Jesus the life changer—was passing through town on the way to Jerusalem.

Everyone was talking about the arrival of the rabbi. Some said that when he spoke publicly, it was as if he had firsthand knowledge of his subject and he taught it with authority. Others said he had a charisma about him that drew you closer, compelled you to listen, and demanded full attention. Still others held that he wasn't just a religious leader, but he was turning the old ways of religion on its head and infuriating those who held to tradition.

And while Zacchaeus didn't seem to be a religious person, he certainly was curious about this newcomer. Jesus was a regional fascination. His popularity as well as his infamy were on the rise. The man from Galilee was a polarizing figure, to be sure, but Zacchaeus hoped to get a glimpse of Jesus as he passed by, maybe see what people saw in him. If he was lucky, he could at least brag to his associates that he witnessed one of Jesus's miracles firsthand.

Associates. That's all he had, really. Imagine the life of a crooked tax collector. It's not likely he had real friends, or at least he didn't hang out with the kind of people that made up real friendships. Zacchaeus's relationships were largely transactional: what-can-you-do-for-me, you-scratch-my-back-I'll-scratch-yours types of arrangements. He had climbed the ladder of success, and on each successive rung he left behind neighbors who felt exploited, friends who felt betrayed, and family members who felt ashamed of what one of their own had become. Zacchaeus was a tax collector; a shill, a heavy, and a thug for the Romans. Raised as a Jew, he had become the ultimate traitor to his heritage and his history. And not only was he a tax collector, he was a *chief* tax collector. He oversaw a major toll collection point in Jericho where every item on the trade route was taxed. Heavy taxes. Unfair taxes. He was the architect of—quite literally—highway robbery. Zacchaeus was the worst of the worst, universally hated by those he had stolen from.

There. Down that street the crowd had mostly come to a standstill and the numbers had swelled. He heard shouts, cheers. From this distance it was hard to tell who was happy to see Jesus and who wanted him to move on to the next village. Zacchaeus started down the alley, trying to visually separate the crowd from the one they were crowding to see. He crouched low. He stood on his tiptoes. He even added in a couple of undignified hops just for good measure.

Nothing.

For all of Zacchaeus's political stature, he had very little physical stature. All of the clout in the world couldn't add to his height, and Zach was a small man indeed. But he wanted just one peek. One glimpse of the local celebrity was all he needed. One glance at the one who was changing the face of Judea. But try as he might, Zacchaeus couldn't get to Jesus because of the crowd.

• • •

In the church world, we all deal with crowds. Oh sure, some crowds are larger than others. Whether you're a sprawling metropolitan megachurch or a small-town storefront start-up, crowds are a part of church life. If you're a church leader, every weekend you have to walk in with a plan to deal with the crowds. Whether it's organizing a fleet of parking shuttles or just feeding another quarter into a parking meter, part of our mission when we gather corporately is to greet and treat people well.

If you look over the landscape of the modern-day church and the small mountain of resources that have been produced on how to *do* church, you will find some disparity when it comes to handling crowds. Some churches love crowds. Some tolerate them. Some view newly arriving guests as an afterthought, and some hold them as the focus of the weekend plan.

Before I continue, I need to take a moment to define what I mean by *crowd*, because after all, if I'm going to be talking about the concept over the course of this book, you need to know *who*

I'm referring to. Back in the mid-1990s Rick Warren wrote a book called *The Purpose Driven Church* (maybe you've heard of it; I hear it sold a few copies). In it he separated the terms *community* and *crowd*.[1] Community—by Warren's definition—is the pool of lost people surrounding your facility who have committed to neither Jesus nor his church. The crowd would involve everyone who actually shows up for a weekend service, believer or not.

I agree with that distinction and that definition, but with a couple of qualifiers. First, we must explicitly state that on any given Sunday, some people are in your crowd for the very first time. They have made their way from the community, having deliberately chosen to accept an invitation, seek out a church, "find religion," or act on any number of motivations that has made them take a step—toward friendship, Jesus, meaning, purpose, whatever. And there is a substantial difference between a first-time guest and a second-time guest. A first-timer is seeing everything with new eyes. They're absorbing it all, processing it all, and yes, even critiquing it all. A second-timer—though still doing a lot of processing—has made an internal shift. As Nelson Searcy says, "Many first-time guests are dragged into church by someone else. . . . When they decide to return for a second time, it's usually out of their own volition."[2]

So we must not forget that every weekend is someone's first weekend. Remembering this raises the stakes for those who continue Jesus's work. It reminds us of the importance of treating every member of the crowd as if it's their first time, because for some it is. But that raises the second qualifier, which is acknowledging the razor-thin edge between crowd and community. One minute before a guest steps onto your church property, they are a part of the community. And if you do a poor job of welcoming them, if they feel ignored or unloved, if you don't proceed with due diligence in following up with them and building a relationship with them, they will go right back to being a part of the community. No second chances. No do-overs. You have one opportunity to bring them into the fold, and unless you steward that opportunity well, they may not ever come back.

So while I am grateful for Warren's *crowd* definition, I think we must pay special attention to the newest fringes of the crowd. Are your longtime members important? Yep. Should you pay attention to the faithful who have been there for decades? You betcha. Does every person who shows up every weekend deserve to be treated with grace and dignity? Absolutely. But I'm afraid that we can love those whom we know to the detriment of those whom we don't yet know. Our attention doesn't have to be on either/or. The thrust of this book is to elevate intentionality toward those coming for the first time, but also to show that intentionality can't just be driven by the staff; it must be championed by the congregation. We must raise the guest awareness culture in our churches so our fifty-year veterans can demonstrate the love of Jesus to those who have been around for five minutes.

As long as I am defining things, let me toss in my intentions for one more term. You will notice that throughout these pages, I use the word *guest* quite liberally. I use it to refer to anyone who shows up at your church at any time. Charter member or first-timer, out-of-towner or longtime neighbor, lead pastor or brand-new volunteer—they all are your guests and should be treated as such. Thinking of everyone as a guest changes the mind-set of a congregation. Right here at the beginning of the book, I beg you to steer clear of the dreaded "*v* word." Don't label people as *visitors*, honor them as *guests*. As Gary McIntosh wisely puts it, "There is a difference. . . . Visitors are often unwanted; guests are expected. Visitors just show up; guests are invited. Visitors are expected to leave; guests are expected to stay. Visitors come one time; guests return again."[3]

So there are *guests*, and then there are *first-time guests*. I'll do my best to explicitly state the difference as we go. And in both of those categories, we'll have even more subcategories. You'll likely encounter a hodgepodge of believers, nonbelievers, saints, skeptics, hostiles, agnostics, atheists, unconvinced, and seekers.[*][4]

TWO TYPES OF CHURCHES

Before we jump ahead, let's return to the original question: How do churches respond to crowds? More specifically, how does *your* church respond to crowds? What is the typical mind-set when it comes to dealing with the guests God sends your way? The range of answers is as varied as the range of churches: no two congregations treat their guests in exactly the same way. But for the purposes of this introduction, I'm going to pull out a really broad brush and paint caricatures of two types of churches and their respective views of caring for guests. I know, I know: the "broad brush" thing is dangerous. I am running the risk of mislabeling churches and maligning friends. But hang on until the end of the paint job and I'll attempt to bring some balance to the conversation. (Either that or just go online right now and write a hostile review.[†])

Church type number one is the "Experience Is Superficial" church. We'll call this First United Memorial Church. First United is steeped in tradition. They pride themselves on the old ways of doing church and see themselves as primarily a protective bubble: it's okay by them if they keep the saints in and the sinners out. They like their steeples high and their stained glass conservative.

---

[*] The nineties called. They want their church-growth term back.
[†] Please don't.

They tend to be heavy on doctrine and light on delight. Emotional expression during a church service is frowned upon. A guest service team would be just so many bells and whistles because, after all, guests don't need frills—they just need Jee-*EEE*-sus. (If you didn't grow up in the South, allow me to translate: "Jesus." The more traditional you are, the more syllables he gets. It also helps if you have a little sweat on your upper lip as you bellow his name.)

While we might consider First United as a bubble, they would claim they are anything but. "We just love everybody" might be a common theme. They have an active outreach ministry in the community. They are genuinely concerned about the lost souls in the shadow of their steeple and truly want to see people come to faith in Christ. And yet their plan of action doesn't reflect love so much as self-protection. In their well-placed and well-intentioned struggle to elevate their teaching and hold on to their values, they often fail to take into consideration the "outsider" in their midst. So while they give careful attention to what they *say*, they give little attention to what a guest *hears*. They may indeed preach truth, but they don't accompany it with relational love. Hospitality is effectively ignored in deference to the "serious business" of worship, and a guest is left feeling underwhelmed by the experience.

Church type number two is the "Experience Is Central" church. In some ways they are a reaction to the traditional church. There are no stuffy-sounding names here, so we'll call this fellowship "Tribe." (Not "Tribe Church." Not "The Tribe." Just "Tribe." One pundit says that if your church can't be confused with a designer jeans store, you're doing it wrong.[5]) Tribe meets in a renovated warehouse. Their pastor wears skinny jeans.* Sometimes he preaches from a stool. He's completely bald but has a beard that would make ZZ Top

---

* Full disclosure: I'm a pastor who wears skinny jeans, just not on purpose. I suspect it has something to do with the nightly bowl of ice cream.

jealous. And Tribe is all about—well, adding you to their tribe. So they pull out all the stops: handcrafted, fair-trade coffee stations. Rockin' band. Parking shuttles. Swirly slides at kids' check-in. They want to impact the world for Jesus, so they're going to do whatever it takes to make you feel welcome and to get you back.

But there's a drawback to Tribe's approach as well. Because they put such an emphasis on experience, they avoid anything that would derail the experience. They are careful to design each step in a way that the feelings of their community come first. They walk on eggshells when it comes to saying or doing anything that would draw a line in the cultural sand. They pay attention to every detail, but in doing so they overlook one crucial detail, and that is that the gospel must inform everything. Usually it's not overt: They craft series around felt needs rather than the exposition of Scripture. In an attempt to show everyone how welcome they are, they relax standards for membership and accommodate lifestyles that aren't yielded to the lordship of Jesus. And in the end, they end up with a very friendly place that is fairly hostile toward gospel truth.

As one author succinctly says, "Many congregations are quite adept at proclaiming the gospel but very inept at welcoming and assimilating people. Others may be very successful at welcoming and receiving new members but seldom proclaim the gospel."[6]

See? I warned you that I'd be painting these two types of churches with a broad brush. And maybe that didn't bother you too much when you were reading the caricature of the "other guy." You sit on the opposite side of the fence from a church like First United Memorial and you're still chuckling over the "they like their stained glass conservative" line.* You know churches like that in your city, and you know they aren't doing a great job of invading the

---

* Ain't gonna lie. I'm particularly proud of that one.

darkness because they're so busy huddling in the light. Or maybe you know of a church exactly like Tribe, and you're suspicious of their lack of commitment to theology and their reckless grab for relevancy. You're afraid they have traded in historical Christian tradition for a gimmick-filled sermonette, and you're afraid that if the unbelievers of your town attend that church, they'll be no better off than if they had simply stayed home.

But before you get upset over my characterizations*—or allow yourself to be painted into one particular corner—recognize that a little bit of both First United and Tribe exists in all of us. Rarely can we find a church that falls completely in one camp or another. To assume that seeker-driven churches have no theologians or that tradition-centered churches have no warmth is wildly erroneous. Both sides have strengths and weaknesses. And all of us have our go-to characteristics of the other guys that we like to villainize, when in reality we can carry those elements into our own ministries. We all have blind spots in the way we approach ministry, and we can all acknowledge shortfalls in the model we choose.

The irony is, nobody thinks they are in either extreme. Tribe looks across town at First United and says, "Wow, if a traditional group of stick-in-the-mud fundies ever existed, they're it." Meanwhile, the people at the proverbial First United are thinking, "Well yeah, we're traditional, but we're not nearly as bad as Very First United down the street. Those people still do Gregorian chants." No matter where you fall on the scale, someone believes you're somewhere different on the scale than where you believe you are.

I get it. Broad brushstrokes over differing church models can be frustrating (maybe a little infuriating). My point is that we are *all* the two churches. We all have the tendency to slide into the

---

* "Who's upset? I'M NOT UPSET!" (*throws book across room*)

caricatures we despise. When we eschew tradition and promote our "new ways," we must remember that today's new ways are simply tomorrow's traditions. When we look down on a church that is too accommodating to people's feelings, we have to acknowledge the ineffective ministries in our church that still exist because—well, because we don't want to hurt someone's feelings. Because the people we are trying to reach won't remain static, we can't remain static in our particular approaches to ministry. As their worldview evolves and changes, the way we speak into their lives must change as well. As the old adage goes, we should be rigid with the message but flexible with our methods.

The two parts of this book are set up to address two types of focus our churches must have when it comes to guest services. In part 1, "Looking Out," we'll cover *outward hospitality*: the community-facing ministry of our churches. You'll see the necessity of our corporate worship services being set up with our own cities in mind, the importance of thinking through every detail on behalf of our guests, and the beauty that is experienced when we reclaim hospitality as a gospel apologetic.

In part 2, "Looking In", we'll turn the focus to *inward discipleship*: the gut check we must undergo if we're going to pursue gospel-fueled hospitality. Being less offensive to outsiders may mean that you offend a few insiders. I hope to show you how knowing who you are as a church can affect both outreach and inreach, what to do when your new style of hospitality brings angry people out of the woodwork, and how to help navel-gazers adapt an "others first" mind-set.

As you read, I'll be introducing you to a few seemingly disparate characters. You've already met Zacchaeus, our vertically challenged friend who just wanted a glimpse of Jesus. He'll make recurring appearances throughout the book and will be joined by a media mogul and a self-righteous farm boy. Through these three characters—both biblical and historical—my goal is to show you the varying degrees in how we approach those who are on the outside, and how Jesus embodies the perfect approach.

Throughout the book you'll be challenged to view your weekend attendees as one of the three types of people we commonly find in our congregations. There are *consumers*, those who are a part of Warren's "community or crowd" definition. These are the people we're called to reach, the ones who don't yet have a relationship with Christ or his church. Don't get too hung up on the *consumers* term just yet; I'll cover it in more detail in chapter 1. There are also *communers*, the card-carrying members of the church. These are your pew dwellers, your faithful, your regulars. They have strong relationships with one another, they are usually strong givers, and in many ways they serve as the backbone of your congregation. And finally, there are the *commissioned*. Leaving people in one of the first two categories is never enough. To truly be a church on mission, we have to move from "What's in it for me?" to "Who is the Holy Spirit calling me to befriend?" (While we might view "consumers" as spiritually immature, the "What's in it for me?" question is a natural one for those entering our churches with baggage from the past.)

As we move through these two areas of focus and three types of people, I pray that God would open our eyes to see clearly where we stand. My goal is that we will recognize both where we are and where our congregations are. If people are the mission, then let us blaze a trail to show that guest-centric and gospel-centric churches are not at opposite ends of the spectrum. Honoring the stranger doesn't stand at odds with honoring the Savior. People are indeed the mission that Christ has called us to, and if we focus on people, we can help people focus on the gospel.

• • •

And behold, there was a man named Zacchaeus. He was a chief tax collector and was rich. And he was seeking to see who Jesus was, but on account of the crowd he could not. (Luke 19:2–3)

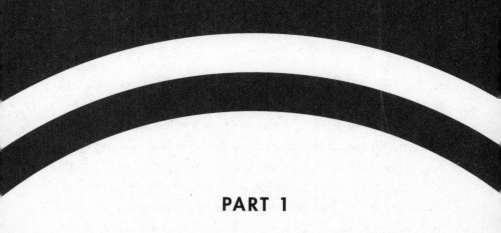

PART 1

LOOKING OUT

The crowd refused to move, and Zacchaeus refused to leave. He could just barely see the top of Jesus's head: one moment the celebrity was bending down to touch someone who couldn't stand, the next he was lifting a squealing, giggling toddler into the air. And all of this made Zacchaeus all the more desperate to see Jesus. So with a quick calculation of the miracle worker's next move, he decided to get ahead of the crowd for an up-close view.

But the crowd had the same idea. With every step forward, more people appeared. Throngs came out of homes, out of businesses, out of side streets, out of nowhere and everywhere all at the same time to investigate the fuss, noise, shouting, and jubilation. Elbows and rumps and bobbing heads wedged Zacchaeus out and drove his frustration deeper. This was his now-or-never moment. He was going to catch a glimpse of Jesus one way or another.

If you asked him later, I wonder what Zacchaeus would have said about his encounter with Jesus. Would he have remembered the details of hiking up his robe and planting his foot on the trunk of the tree? Could he accurately replay his thought process of getting from ground level to above-the-crowd level? Maybe he would tell you he's not sure how he scaled the first few feet of the trunk to reach the bottom branch. Perhaps he would remark that he's never been a tree climber. That people like him shouldn't be tree climbers. That tax collectors—*chief* tax collectors, especially—shouldn't be tree climbers. People like him certainly don't shimmy up trees. But desperate chief tax collectors like Zacchaeus sometimes throw caution to the wind and end up shimmying anyway. They let their desires win out over their dignity.

I'd guess that what Zacchaeus *could* tell you was that there was a brief moment—right after he perched on that limb but right before Jesus came into view—when his adrenaline gave way to apprehension. He could remember vividly the moment of doubt, the moment of self-consciousness, the moment when he looked around to see just how many people were watching, laughing, pointing at, whispering about, and snickering over the little man in the tree. He would tell you that even in his mental postmortem of the moment, he wasn't sure what he expected to gain by seeing Jesus. He just knew that he *wanted* to see him.

• • •

We're surrounded by people like Zacchaeus. Every day we bump elbows with people in a state of desperation. Granted, most wouldn't describe it that way; in fact, most would deny that description. After all, they don't *feel* desperate. They're happy with their lifestyle and with their choices. Nevertheless, even they might admit that something always feels a bit off, something seems to be missing, something rings a bit hollow. Sometimes that emptiness shows up in the pursuit of more. Perhaps it's more relationships, more stuff, more job status, more free time, more cash in the bank. Maybe it's an adrenaline-fueled rush that causes the modern-day Zacchaeus to plant his foot on the trunk of a tree and start climbing and see . . . *something* . . . experience something, own something, gain something that will patch the emptiness.

People may tell you what they *want*: security. Safety. Status. Love. A sense of belonging. Freedom. Self-fulfillment. What they can't often articulate is what they *need*: the deeper holes that can't be filled by the stuff of earth. And that's not just the proverbial "them." It's all of us. We tend to be a bit myopic when it comes to our wants versus our needs, our *what's near* versus *what's best*. Often we find ourselves sitting on a tree branch second-guessing our last move and trying to guess the next one. Self-fulfillment is precluded by self-consciousness as we furtively look around to see who is staring at us, judging us, laughing at us, taking pity on us.

Sometimes those tree-branch moments lead people on a spiritual journey, one in which they are looking for hope in religion or in God or in a new set of moral codes. And sometimes that journey takes them to church. Not "Church," as in capital *C* church, the Church universal, but "church," the building down the street from their house, the gathering their coworker has been pestering them to attend, the place where they hope they can get things sorted out and maybe clear their heads and perhaps find some answers.

When they come, what do they see? When they encounter the crowd, will they have a clear view? When they perch on their tree branch, will they look down just to see people looking up who are really looking down on them?

Those are the questions that those of us inside the church may ask about the proverbial "them" outside of the church. But if you're a church person—an insider—maybe the better question for you and for me is this: How are we doing at looking out for the outsider?

➔ CHAPTER 1

The Gospel Is Offensive. Nothing Else Should Be

We live in a society where people are easily offended.

We tend to get riled up over just about anything: political scandals, social justice, dietary preferences. Song lyrics, public school curriculum, beer commercials. Cultural norms, water cooler conversations, social media posts. From animal rights to abortion and global warming to gluten sensitivities, we all have a hill that we're willing to die on and we can't wait to throw a verbal punch at anyone who may disagree.

I'm not sure when it became fashionable to get our collective jumpers in a bunch over every potential disagreement that's out there. Maybe I should start by blaming my own generation.* I hit my elementary school stride in the late 1970s and early '80s. Those of us on the tail end of Gen X started well. We ushered out the era of Brady Bunch collars and bell-bottoms (you're welcome). We said good-bye to lava lamps and hello to Cabbage Patch Kids (I'm sorry). We were the Coke versus Pepsi generation, the kids who saw Reagan get shot and the *Challenger* explode, the group who was scared to death of nuclear war when we weren't too busy

---

* Sorry guys. Our parachute pants looked awesome, though.

hurling our Rubik's Cubes across the shag-carpeted living room in frustration.

But we may also have been the first generation to grow up in Bubble Wrap. Somewhere along the line we stopped riding our bikes in the streets after dark and started barricading ourselves behind closed doors while scary news shows told us about the scary things we didn't know we should be scared of. When we scraped a knee, we no longer were told just to rub some dirt on it or walk it off, but also to get booster shots to ward off infection and maybe toss in an MRI for good measure.

And beyond the basics of safety and health, we somehow stumbled into Bubble-Wrapping our *feelings*. We were inspired to find our inner voice. We were told that we were special and unique.[*] We started using terms like *self-esteem* and *personal worth*. We were told that we were snowflakes.

Precious.

If I'm honest, a part of me understands this. As a parent of four children, I think there's merit in cautiously guiding our kids and leading ourselves in a world gone mad. But can you agree with me that we've gone a little overboard? You don't have to spend more than a few minutes on Facebook or in the comments section on any webpage to discover that the Bubble-Wrapped generation has grown up. We lurk in the shadows, watching for an opportunity to get our feelings hurt over some poorly worded phrase or poorly executed campaign. We apply our politically correct rules and postmodern assessments to decide what will and will not fly in regard to culture, religion, whatever. We cry "foul" over the slightest hint of the slightest offense that may or may not be out there waiting to squash our inner voice and threaten the fragility of our self-esteem.

---

[*] Just like everyone else.

We've even invented a word for these offenses: *microaggressions*. It's a term that sounds almost adorable, like a tiny teacup Chihuahua with huge eyes and a high-pitched bark. Except that when you offend the Chihuahua you realize that he represents a consortium of pit bulls and Rottweilers who would love nothing more than to chew your face off and then publicly shame you in the media.

Keeping up with the terminology we're supposed to use has almost become a game. I can never remember if I should call my congresspersons to complain about the challenges facing the underresourced persons of size who may be dietetically impaired, or if that's more a conversation I have with my significant other gender-different life partner.*

Here's the point: people get offended over lots of things. I certainly have my own proclivities that you might find silly. Some of you may have already gotten offended at this chapter, and we're just a couple of pages in.† We may be able to do little to counter the offenses people decide to take on, but we can certainly do our part not to add to the pile.

There is a flip side of the offense coin, and that's the "make everybody happy" issue of tolerance. American culture loves tolerance. It's the buzzword that keeps school systems in line and fuels politicians' speeches. Because tolerance is so easy—except when it's not. Like when people aren't tolerant of the things we want them to be tolerant of. And when the tolerance police refuse to tolerate those who don't show tolerance, then it just gets silly.

When it comes to *religious* tolerance, John Piper has this to say:

Once upon a time tolerance was the power that kept lovers of competing faiths from killing each other. It was the principle

---

* Not that there's anything wrong with that.
† Please don't ask for a refund. I'll behave. I promise.

that put freedom above forced conversion. It was rooted in the truth that coerced conviction is no conviction. That is true tolerance. But now the new professional tolerance denies that there *are* any competing faiths; they only complement each other. It denounces not only the effort to force conversions but also the idea that any conversion may be necessary. It holds the conviction that no religious conviction should claim superiority over another. In this way, peaceful parity among professionals can remain intact, and none need be persecuted for the stumbling block of the cross (Gal. 5:11).[1]

Churches should be a safe place for the offended and a challenging place for the tolerant. The weekend gathering should point people beyond their preferences and peculiarities and to the life-changing power of God. It should be a time when we collectively come together to see that our individual story is just a tiny speck in the grander story of God's design for humanity. When the people of God assemble, it should be less about grumbling, less about "Let's all just get along," and more about the grandeur of Jesus.

There's just one small problem.

Typically, church people are among the worst when it comes to taking offense. We *love* to get offended when our nonbelieving friends and neighbors say or do anything that we perceive as an attack on our faith. We are quick to cry, "Persecution!" when our employer kindly asks us to stop passing out tracts or a Christian movie gets a bad review after a public release.* We are quick to ostracize our friends when their political proclivities don't line up toe to toe with our religious persuasion. In an age of outrage, we've forgotten the subtle, fragrant aroma of graciousness.

---

* "You hated that movie because it was Christian!" "No, I hated it because the writing, acting, dialogue, photography, and special effects were so awful they'd make baby Jesus cry."

That's why it can be hard for us to see how Christian culture—and more specifically, our weekend gatherings—can be perceived as offensive to those on the outside. Because of our thin skin, we tend to view the weekend worship experience as our refuge from the world. We get to sing our songs, listen to our stories, sit in our pews, and do things our way. We fence ourselves off and barricade ourselves in against those evildoers on the outside. And we are a people who have become familiarly comfortable with the way we do things. Our traditions—for good or for bad—are *our* traditions.

But we need to avoid assuming that because churches are modern, progressive, or cutting edge, they're any less traditional. Though you may slap new paint on old ways and give them a different name, you can still become entrenched in the way things are done in your particular fellowship. A drum set can be as much of a sacred cow as a pipe organ. Small groups can become as untouchable as Sunday school. And for that reason, we tend to protect our methods pretty fiercely. We dress them up in robes and liturgy. We modernize and rebrand them. We hold on to history or blaze new trails. Whatever you do, you probably are doing it because you think that's the best way. It's *your* way.

But is it something your surrounding community can understand? If someone comes into your church as a first-time guest, can they break through those traditions, decipher the secret handshake, and figure out your cultural code? Are your weekend services set up to serve you and those like you, or are they set up so guests see Jesus on display and are invited to engage with him? Do you meet people where they are, or must they work to crack the perimeter and get inside? We must remember that what is traditional for insiders can prove confusing for outsiders.

Is your church a chasm for seekers or a catalyst to Jesus?

Answering this question in a way that is welcoming to those

on the outside means learning to deal with offenses. If people are offended by their experience at your church, they aren't likely to give you a second hearing. If their offense is at the forefront, then the message of the gospel fades into the background. You can resource thousands of dollars, dozens of leaders, and hundreds of volunteers for an excellent weekend experience, but if a guest is offended by what you say before the service, what you do during the service, or how you do it, you may never get a chance to build a relationship with them. Worse, you may turn them off to a relationship with Jesus.

OFFENSES MATTER

"Hang on," you might say.* "Are you proposing that we have to anticipate and respond to every offense out there? Have you read the first part of your own chapter? People get offended over *everything*. How can a church possibly cater to every personality quirk and oversensitive soul that comes through our doors?"

Your objection is a valid one, and we'll unpack it in just a moment. But before we get there, we have to acknowledge that offenses really do matter. These are real issues for real people. You don't have to agree with those issues. You don't even have to understand them. You just have to realize they're out there and they could be the thing that drives a person away from your church.

When my oldest son Jacob was just a little guy, he was terrified of people in costumes. Minor league ball games, Disney World, store grand openings—any place that had a character in an oversized head would send him into a panic. One year we took him to Chuck E. Cheese's for his birthday. Bad mistake. Every twenty

---

* Why are you talking out loud to a book? That's weird.

minutes an oversized rodent with massive teeth emerged from backstage to the delight of kids throughout the restaurant. Well, all of the kids besides Jacob, who had barricaded himself beneath the table and had a death grip on my shins.

Try as we might, we couldn't convince Jacob that there was a real person in that mouse costume. We would prep him to meet the mouse, explain to him that there was nothing to be afraid of, try to ease into the encounter from across the room. It didn't matter. We were guaranteed that somewhere between the last slice of pepperoni pizza and the first token in the Skee-Ball machine, our son was going to be flat on the floor in sheer terror.*

Seeing all of this as an adult, I knew that my son's fear was irrational. I knew that Chuck E. was likely a kid working his way through college from the interior of a rat suit. I knew that he would do my child no harm and was probably more scared of him than the other way around. But to Jacob, his fear was real. The offense was tangible. And it wasn't going away just because I couldn't understand it.†

The same is true for guests at your church. There are things that you do that offend, bother, or irritate them, and you can't simply write off their offenses, their prejudices, and their preconceived ideas. And make no mistake: guests can and will object over everything from intolerance to inattention, from doctrinal stances to denominational practices. They will get offended over phrases you use, rudeness they perceive, or a spirit of narrow-mindedness they sense in the way you speak and act. Regardless of whether you think their objections are justified, *they are still their objections.* They are real issues for real people, and you really have to acknowledge and

---

* "Happy birthday, son. Here's a gift card for a future therapy session."

† Fast-forward a dozen years to Jacob's first job, where he had a stint at a local Chick-fil-A as their cow mascot. The Lord indeed works in moo-steer-i-ous ways.

understand them if you hope to project a welcoming environment for your guests and greet them with the hospitality of the gospel.

If people are the mission, then dealing with those objections and offenses are all a part of the mission.

Not long ago a family visited our church for the first time. If maritime accidents could be compared to a guest experience, this was the sinking of the *Titanic*. They arrived late—well after the service started—and because our team had already been reduced to a skeleton crew, they had a hard time finding convenient parking. They dropped their preschool-aged children off to a busy classroom that was already under way. They had missed a good portion of the service, so they had no idea what was happening or why. There was no context to help them acclimate to what was happening. And shortly after they were seated, their infant needed a diaper change. Mom walked the length of our building, looking in vain for a changing station. When she went to check on her preschool child in the kids' area, she was told she couldn't enter without her pickup tag, which she had left in the auditorium. As you might guess, it all ended with Mom having an emotional blowup directed toward a kids' staff person and a clear declaration that this was the worst experience she had ever had anywhere.

Let's analyze this experience, shall we? Our team blew it on some points; and the guests didn't do themselves any favors on others. *First, the guests were late, then angry when they couldn't find front-row parking and preferred seating.* "It's their own fault!" you say. Well, sure. But we could have done a much better job coming alongside them as they got out of the car, acting as advocates rather than being aggravated that they were late. *Second, Mom couldn't find a changing table.* "Well, why didn't she ask someone?" you say. Again, good point. But on the flip side, we could have been proactive in watching for people who left the service and needed a hand. Had we been on the ball, she would have known that a changing table was just a few feet across the lobby in the restrooms. *Third, Mom was upset over the delay in checking on her preschooler.* "But we had good reason for not allowing her back with the kids!" And yes, we did. But we could have led in our response with some assistance ("I'd be happy to walk back with you") rather than the rules ("Without a pickup sticker, you can't come back here by yourself"). We could have helped her to see why our actions were actually for the good of her child.

Are our security procedures for the children's area important? You bet. Can we hold the start of the service for someone who will be twenty minutes late? Not likely. But even in our structure, we can design an experience that accommodates people who need a little extra assistance. Our guests in this scenario were already having a bad morning and were probably more prone to spot the problems. But here is the key point we need to remember: *if we are ministering to our guests out of a gospel-centric mind-set, we won't just react.* We'll lead with grace in an attempt to demonstrate the kindness of Jesus.

Ignoring the potential to offend is itself offensive. It communicates to people that you care more about protecting your old ways than preparing for guests. It rings of exclusivity, not inclusivity. It gives guests a reason to write off your church, because you are giving them exactly what they expect: you are internally focused, unfriendly, shut off from the outside world.

BE OFFENDED OVER THE RIGHT THINGS

But let me be clear. I'm not trying to convince you that your worship services or your church structure should become a sterile environment where you don't take stands on important issues or where you never proclaim absolutes. Neutrality leads to all sorts of doctrinal rabbit holes where universalism reigns and truth is abstract. No. Certain things about some church services will offend some people. There's no getting around that. I'm simply arguing that we decide to be strategic about *how* and *why* we offend people. We want them to be offended over the right things. As Tim Keller says, "This is not avoiding the bold proclamation of the truth; rather, it is *leading* with the offense of the gospel instead of with the truths that are predicated on the gospel."[2]

And when we read the Gospels, we see that Jesus did just that. You can scarcely read any chapter in Matthew, Mark, Luke, or John without realizing that a large part of Jesus's ministry involved alienating the people around him. The religious types hated him. The Romans didn't understand him. His brothers didn't believe in him. Even his disciples said that his teachings were difficult and hard to believe.[*]

So Jesus didn't operate out of a "Let's just all get along" mentality. He said that he had come to set a man against his father, a daughter against her mother, and a daughter-in-law against her mother-in-law (Matthew 10:35). He had a habit of showing up at pastors conferences and giving them affectionate nicknames like hypocrites, children of hell, blind guides, whitewashed tombs, and vipers (Matthew 23). He labeled one of his closest friends Satan and his Jewish brethren the sons of the devil (Mark 8:33; John 8:44). The red letters of the New Testament bleed with patently offensive declarations said by a man we call the Prince of Peace.

But Jesus's offensive statements weren't accidental. They had a purpose. He used offense to shock the self-righteous with their own depravity, to give the hopeless outsiders a glimpse of hope, and to turn a centuries-old religious system on its head as he ushered

---

[*] Youth pastors, take heart: you're more like Jesus than you thought.

in a new kingdom. That couldn't be done by tiptoeing around the real problems with the religious establishment. It couldn't be implemented through seven steps to Your Best Judaism Now. The problems couldn't be solved by avoiding conflict and embracing political correctness. Jesus not only embodied truth, he spoke truth. And the truth that he spoke frequently offended and sometimes cut deep.

Consider the account recorded in Luke 4:14–30. Jesus had recently returned from the wilderness, where he had fasted for forty days and endured temptations hurled at him by Satan. Now he was starting his pulpit supply ministry in Galilee, going from synagogue to synagogue to teach on the Sabbath. Scripture tells us that as he taught, he was being "glorified by all" (v. 15) and gaining popularity in the region. He was the hot new speaker on the Jewish circuit: all the conference organizers were knocking at his door, publicists lined up to represent him, and publishers drafted up book deals. Hebrew bookstores had already designed the coffee mugs with his face on them. Everybody wanted on the Jesus bandwagon.

And when he showed up in his hometown of Nazareth, it was no different. One Sabbath morning Jesus was attending services with his family. I imagine that Mary, being a good Jewish mother, elbowed him as he sat beside her in the pew and whispered, "Such a good boy you are. You should go up there and read the scroll. Rebecca's son read the scroll last week. You know I've always loved to hear you read the scroll."

So Jesus stood up, walked down front, took the scroll of Isaiah off of the scroll shelf, and began to read:

> "The Spirit of the Lord is upon me,
>   because he has anointed me
>   to proclaim good news to the poor.

He has sent me to proclaim liberty to the captives
and recovering of sight to the blind,
to set at liberty those who are oppressed,
to proclaim the year of the Lord's favor." (Luke 4:18–19)

And then he sat down. What follows is one of the most dramatic sentences in the New Testament:

And the eyes of all in the synagogue were fixed on him. (v. 20)

Silence. Not a word was spoken. It was a holy moment. Somewhere beneath a bench, a cricket chirped.

Jesus, sensing the tension and feeling the stares, looked up, made eye contact with those around him, and spoke again, deliberately, slowly: "Today this Scripture has been fulfilled in your hearing" (v. 21).

This would have been the moment that I would have chosen to drop the scroll and walk offstage, but I trust that Jesus knew what he was doing. Verse 22 tells us that the crowd ate that right up: "All spoke well of him and marveled at the gracious words that were coming from his mouth. And they said, 'Is this not Joseph's son?'"

The hometown boy had made them proud. Jesus, the boy next door. Jesus, the son of the carpenter. Something about his demeanor as he read, something about his graciousness as he spoke, something about his humility intermingled with authority grabbed the attention of the crowd. Whispers began to echo through the meeting space: "I knew he'd make something of himself one day." "I bet he's going to do great things." "His brother James should aspire to be more like him."

And then, seizing an opportunity to take it one step further and shake up their Sabbath, he spoke again:

"Doubtless you will quote to me this proverb, '"Physician, heal yourself." What we have heard you did at Capernaum, do here in your hometown as well.'" And he said, "Truly, I say to you, no prophet is acceptable in his hometown. But in truth, I tell you, there were many widows in Israel in the days of Elijah, when the heavens were shut up three years and six months, and a great famine came over all the land, and Elijah was sent to none of them but only to Zarephath, in the land of Sidon, to a woman who was a widow. And there were many lepers in Israel in the time of the prophet Elisha, and none of them was cleansed, but only Naaman the Syrian." (vv. 23–27)

In other words, "Truth has come to Nazareth. The Messiah is here. A prophet stands in your midst. You've had other prophets, a string of them, but you've rejected them. Remember Elijah? He could have fed all the widows of Bethel, but they wouldn't believe. Remember Elisha? He could have healed all of the lepers in Israel, but your lack of faith prevented it. And so the God of Israel gave his food to a Sidonian and his grace to a Syrian." In one fell swoop, Jesus told the chosen people that God was taking his blessing beyond their borders. He was expanding his reach to the people the chosen people hated. He was going from the promised land to the land inhabited by so-called infidels and foreigners.

Okay, so maybe *that* was the time to drop the scroll. The crowd gasped. His brothers' mouths hung open. The presiding rabbi canceled the closing worship song. And pandemonium ensued in the place where Jesus had grown up. The man who had been Nazareth's favorite son a few moments earlier was now public enemy number one. The crowd at the synagogue seethed with wrath and seized the heretic, buying him a one-way ticket out of town and escorting him to a scenic drop off the nearest cliff.

I have to assume he never got his honorarium check.

Jesus didn't let the history and tradition of his Hebrew audience stand in the way of truth. He didn't allow niceties and social graces to interfere with the revolution. Standing on this side of the gospel story, it's easy to excuse Jesus's words that day because we know they were necessary and true. But that didn't make them less offensive to his hearers.

My guess is that two thousand years later you still have a few bruised Jews in your pews. What I mean is that every weekend the truth claims of Jesus rub people the wrong way. Rather than seeing him as the prophet he is, they see him as a good teacher. Rather than the sacrifice for our sins, they see a role model. Rather than a revolutionary, they see a rabble-rouser. The masses still want a neatly packaged Jesus who will sit in the corner and behave himself, not a sovereign Lord who will disrupt their lives.

Rather than *the* Way, they want *a* way.

Note, however, that this misinterpretation of Jesus doesn't catch him off guard. He's not wringing his hands in heaven, hoping we'll launch a better public relations campaign and push his name up a few points in the opinion polls. While he established the church and left it in the hands of his apostles as the primary catalyst for the Great Commission, he's not depending on our savvy marketing, slick brochures, and cutting edge LED screens to make him more palatable to modern society. As a matter of fact, sometimes our marketing serves to *detract* from the message of Jesus rather than *attract* people to it.

Exhibit A: judgment houses.

You might remember judgment houses. They were all the rage of 1990s youth group culture. Every year at Halloween, churches would transform fellowship halls and Sunday school rooms and auditoriums into a walk-through drama where melodramatic actors played out a story line intended to showcase the horrors of hell and the glories of heaven.

Judgment houses followed a fairly predictable formula: Character 1 (popular cheerleader who met Jesus at Bible camp) and Character 2 (party-loving jock who has no time for religion) encounter Really Bad Situation (car wreck). Cue the next scene (hospital emergency room outfitted with a loaner ambulance) where the demons show up to drag Character 2 to hell (fellowship hall with lots of screaming; heat turned up to ninety degrees) and the angels escort Character 1 to heaven (auditorium with lots of white taffeta, gold tinsel halos, and Third Day playing in the background).

My problem with judgment houses is not the poorly written script, poorly acted scenes, or poorly decorated rooms (though all of those could spark another chapter in this book). No, my issue is that for every one person who came to faith during a judgment house, there were likely a hundred who walked away shaking their heads and rolling their eyes at the perceived corniness of Christianity. Where we meant well, I'm afraid that we simply reinforced the skeptics' belief that Jesus is for out-of-touch people with too much time and taffeta on their hands.

Now I realize that we could make that argument with just about any initiative the church has undertaken in its two-thousand-year history. (Remember the Crusades? Those were fun.) I'm not picking on judgment houses per se. Someone reading this might have been the one out of a hundred who came to faith at a judgment house.* Someone else might have prayed to receive Jesus after eating the cheap butter cookies and drinking the warm Kool-Aid of a

---

* I actually have a friend who became a believer at one of those "Jesus versus Satan" overdramatized exhibitions in a wrestling ring. (Spoiler: Jesus gets knocked out, but wait for it. . . .)

local vacation Bible school. Still another reader might have been convicted of their sins after reading a brilliantly worded church marquee.*

My point is that the modern American church doesn't always display the cultural savvy and rhetorical genius of the apostle Paul at the Areopagus. Too many times we try to dress up the gospel in trendy clothes and catchy phrases intended to make it more attractive. We fear that the gospel—left to itself—will be unable to stand on its own.

Charles Spurgeon had something to say about that. The nineteenth-century Baptist preacher must have been to one too many judgment houses in his day. Of the gospel, Spurgeon remarked,

> The Word of God can take care of itself, and will do so if we preach it, and cease defending it. See you that lion. They have caged him for his preservation; shut him up behind iron bars to secure him from his foes! See how a band of armed men have gathered together to protect the lion. What a clatter they make with their swords and spears! These mighty men are intent upon defending a lion. O fools, and slow of heart! Open that door! Let the lord of the forest come forth free. Who will dare to encounter him? What does he want with your guardian care? Let the pure gospel go forth in all its lion-like majesty, and it will soon clear its own way and ease itself of its adversaries.[3]

In other words, when it comes to the gospel, you simply let the lion do what a lion does.

---

* I'm kidding, of course. Church signs are pretty much worthless, except for the fundamental truth that God Answers Knee Mail.

But before we loose the lion, think for a moment about the message of the gospel. Think about what the church puts on display to an unbelieving world. Think about what we as Christians express to our non-Christian friends and family. The gospel is the good news that God has done for us what we cannot do for ourselves, by dying in our place for our sin so that through him we can have eternal life. This offer of salvation is available to all who seek it by repentance and faith. So if the gospel is true, then we can't preach an "I'm okay, you're okay" message. We can't simply choose to coexist. We can't all get up the same mountain on different paths.

No, the Bible proclaims that Jesus is the way, and the truth, and the life, and no one comes to the Father except through him (John 14:6). The Bible teaches that every man, woman, and child under heaven is a sinner separated from God. Our lying tongues, our cursing mouths, our blood-shedding feet, and our idolatrous hearts cause us to stand condemned (Romans 3:9–18). Our sins not only separate us from God on earth but will eventually separate us for all eternity. Those who do not receive the free gift of Jesus will spend forever in hell (Revelation 20:15).

That's not very touchy-feely. As a matter of fact, it's downright offensive. Paul noted that offense in 1 Corinthians 1:18: "For the message of the cross is foolishness to those who are perishing, but it is God's power to us who are being saved" (HCSB).

Not "nonsensical." *Foolishness.* Not "unclear." *Foolishness.* Not "foggy" or "fuzzy" or "a little bit freaky," but *foolishness.*

The gospel doesn't make sense to people who haven't yet received it.

You haven't forgotten the foolish nature of the gospel, have you? Have you forgotten the mystery and the seeming insanity that an invisible God made his Son visible, wrapped him in flesh, placed him in a virgin's womb, and sent him on mission to earth for thirty-three years?

Have you forgotten that Jesus lived a perfect life, remained 100 percent obedient to his Father, fulfilled his purpose, and went to a cross meant for a criminal?

Have you forgotten that Jesus died? *He died.* He remained cold in the ground until the third day, when God raised him back to life.

Have you forgotten that Jesus died for you? And he died for you because you desperately needed him to. Without his death, without his sacrifice, you and I would remain enemies of God and would eventually be separated from him forever.

You see? Foolishness.

I don't know about the community where you live, but in my community, this message gets weirder with each passing year. Gospel-loving people often find themselves on the receiving end of hateful taunts or harmless eye rolls, all because we believe a message that is increasingly countercultural and offensive.*

Some churches have chosen to soften that offense by watering down the message. Rather than talk about indwelling sin, they talk about shortcomings and character flaws. Rather than present Jesus as the truer and better anything, they present twelve keys to a better you.† The seeker-driven movement has produced quite a few good conversation points and outreach strategies that I would agree with, but one of the frequent shortfalls is that it has caged the lion and robbed the gospel of its power.

Flashy programs and sparkly Sundays will only last so long. As pastor and author Mark Dever says, "What you win them *with* is likely what you'll win them *to*."[4] There's a balance between seeker-friendly, attractional services and a more reformed, fundamental

---

* Can anyone say "Christian blogger comment section"? I knew you could!

† Key #4 is teeth-whitening strips—I'm sure of it.

style of weekend planning. But as that balance is pursued, you have to choose between "I'm okay, you're okay" and checking the length of sinners' hemlines as they come through the door.*

That's why I say that though the gospel offends, nothing else should. By the time a guest gets to their seat and listens to the message being preached, we should have done everything possible to pave the way with rose petals and puppy fur. In other words, we should implement the biblical virtue of hospitality at an institutional level to better proclaim and display the gospel.

For your congregation, that may mean a parking team that attempts to place people in the same zip code as the service they're attending. It may mean a first-time-guest tent staffed with your very best greeters to act as advocates on behalf of the guest. It may mean a team that is trained to anticipate, design, and respond to every part of the guest experience. In some venues it may mean a friendly volunteer serving hot coffee and muffins.† It means an eye-catching, warm and friendly kids' area so that parents don't feel like they're dropping their kids off in a gray cinder-block room lined with 1960s era flannelgraphs.

Some would argue that such accommodating reinforces a me-centered mind-set. But move it from a corporate to a personal level, and you'll see that this argument doesn't wash. God is not glorified in your personal hospitality when you invite someone to your home but give them poor directions, a cold fast-food meal, and a halfhearted conversation while your mangy dog sniffs them from head to toe. You would never treat a guest in your home that way. Why on earth would you treat a guest at your church that way?[5]

The hospitality of a church can remove hurdles to the reception

---

* Too short = you cause others to stumble. Too long = you cause yourself to stumble.
† Not just the muffin stumps. (See also "Seinfeld, Jerry.")

of the gospel and encourage faith. And on the flip side, a cold, unfriendly church contradicts the gospel message.[6]

We don't have to choose between dumbing down the gospel and being self-righteous, sanctimonious jerks. Pastors should continue to preach the unfiltered gospel, running the risk of offending people with their sin and shocking them with the unending love of Jesus. But we should also set the table in such a way that nothing apart from the gospel offends them. You see, the *order* of the gospel is important when it comes to guest services. We lead with grace and love, because it was grace and love that changed our own hearts. We don't ask our guests to clean themselves up before we're willing to love them; we just love them. Seek to create the kind of environment where your guests will say, "I don't necessarily agree with what I heard, but I'll never forget how graciously I was treated." That hospitality-soaked environment can eventually turn cold hearts warm and lead people to Christ.

I've seen this principle illustrated with a couple at our church. Blair and Aubrey didn't grow up in Christian homes. In fact, both of their families are skeptical of the church. So when Blair and Aubrey eventually became believers, their decision to follow Jesus was met with a few eye rolls and whispers of somebody "drinking the Kool-Aid."

In the ensuing years, Blair and Aubrey frequently shared the gospel and invited their parents to church, but they never took the couple up on their offer. Until the first grandchild came along. What invitations and pleas can't always do, a grandbaby usually can. Blair's mom flew in for the weekend and decided to tag along for her grandson's first morning at church. It was a dismal, rainy Sunday. I think *monsoon* is the word I'm looking for. But on that particular morning, we had a team of volunteers armed with umbrellas helping guests get in out of the rain. I'll let Blair pick up the story here:

We were greeted by a parking team member with no umbrella but a smile on his face and a walkie-talkie in his hand, showing us the way to the drop zone in front of the auditorium. We were then greeted (much to my mom's amazement) by a team of folks with umbrellas waiting to help my mom, wife, and infant out of the car and into the church.

Needless to say, my mom was really impressed. This top-shelf level of service continued all the way to our seats on the front left side of the church. There was a special touch of care from door to door.

We talk about the importance of showing God's love from the moment one of the volunteers sees a guest. It could not have been more evident than it was yesterday that the team has really embraced that attitude. It is things like that that make an unbeliever scratch their head and wonder what could make someone go to all that trouble on a Sunday morning. Hopefully this is the first of many revelations my mother has when wondering what is different about Christianity.

Do umbrellas save someone's soul? Nope. Does a smiling, rain-soaked volunteer take the place of the Holy Spirit in convicting someone of their sin? Not a chance. But these moments of displayed grace point to God's grace. They pave the way for the gospel to be clearly heard, and they can serve as a catalyst for people to see Jesus more clearly.

Offenses are real. They matter a great deal. They matter to the people you are trying to reach. They matter to the people you are trying to keep. They matter to a world that needs to recognize that the ultimate offense was their sin that sent Jesus to the cross.

But how do you navigate the very slippery slope that comes with removing all offenses? How do you tiptoe around the feelings of people in order to get to the facts of the gospel? How do you balance the call to gospel faithfulness with the desire for community relevance? We'll begin to unearth that answer in the next chapter.

→ CHAPTER 2

The Sermon Starts in the Parking Lot

The year was 1940, and Walter had a problem.

As the daddy of two young girls, he had a desire to raise them in a good church. He didn't need a lot of bells and whistles, but he did insist on the right fit for his family. He wanted his daughters to look forward to church, not dread it. And it would help if he and his wife could get something out of it along the way.

And so the quest began. Every weekend the family would pull out of the driveway of their Southern California home in search of spiritual community. Sunday after Sunday they tried, and Sunday after Sunday they failed. It wasn't because of a lack of churches in their area; there were plenty. It wasn't because Walter had tunnel vision; it was because the churches he visited seemed to have *no* vision. Rather than one message, the churches in his area seemed to communicate multiple messages. Instead of doing a few things well, they did many things poorly.

The churches that Walter and his family visited appeared to be set up for the first visit only. The underlying, unspoken ethos seemed to be that the leadership just wanted to get you in the door. The only problem was, they had no idea what to do beyond that. The facilities weren't laid out well. It wasn't clear where you were supposed to go or how you were supposed to get there. When Walter and his wife finally managed to find the kids' area and drop off their girls at a classroom, the people who received them were sketchy at best.

In addition to the poor quality of communication and the mixed messages and the broken systems, a general sense of disorder and filthiness pervaded every place they visited. More often than not, he discovered that in many of the facilities, the bathrooms smelled bad, the flower beds boasted overgrown weeds, and every square inch was in desperate need of deep cleaning.

The church volunteers felt more like carnival barkers than people who'd been equipped for the work of the ministry. Walter and his family felt herded more than heard. The greetings they received were at best perfunctory and, at worse, just plain rude or nonexistent. And in the rare cases where his daughters had fun and wanted to go back, he and his wife felt like the experience was limited to their kids. He noticed that at most churches the programming sought to divide families rather than unite them.

This might be a good time to mention that Walter had some background as a pastor. While he had never been the lead guy at any church, he had enough experience to know that what he saw wasn't good enough. He wanted an experience that invited him in rather than drove him away. He wanted a place where his family could engage together. As a father, he believed that his girls deserved better. As a pastor, he knew he could do it better.

He began to dream of a church that would have one central message that would impact lives. He mapped out what it would look like if a church actually gave thought to the guest experience. He thought about the environment, planned the traffic flow, obsessed over the cleanliness, and even envisioned the color of the paint on the walls and the music playing overhead. Walter imagined a place where rather than simply getting people in the door, they would practice hospitality with excellence so that people would look forward to returning again and again.

Walter's critics said it couldn't be done. There was no model for such a church in that part of the country, and maybe no model for it anywhere in the world. Until that point in American evangelical history, churches had always seemed to get by on the bare minimum, focusing only on the moment and not the momentum they could have if they actually had a plan and a process to care for people. It seemed like too much show and not enough substance. Even his wife told him that he was biting off more than he could chew. "Why on earth would you undertake something like this?" she asked him. "All of these churches that we've visited are lifeless."

"That's just the point," Walter replied. "This one won't be."

Over the next few years, Walter threw himself into the vision with the passion of a man who couldn't be stopped. He researched possible locations, interviewed potential guests, and raised the money necessary to plant his first church. Fifteen years after his vision began to take shape, the dream became a reality. The buzz surrounding his soft launch was beyond anything he could have hoped, and he was optimistic about what the public perception would be.

That optimism was well placed. The public seemed to embrace Walter's vision before they were able to see it for themselves. They caught previews of the church courtesy of the press, who were fascinated by and wrote extensively about this new concept. One local writer said that Walter was getting ready to "roll up the curtain on the impossible. . . . It [is] costing him sweat and sleeplessness, but he [is] loving every minute of it." That same writer called the church "a dream come true."[1]

July 18, 1955, was launch day, and guests showed up in huge

numbers. In fact, it was nearly triple the crowd Walter had expected. On that first day, there were traffic jams, the refreshments ran out, and his team had to scramble to figure out how to accommodate the overflowing crowd. Southern California was in the grip of a heat wave, and the parking lot asphalt was so soft that ladies' high heels were sinking.

But those minor setbacks just caused Walter and his team to tweak systems even more to create a great experience for their guests. And as they focused on one message and their care for people, people kept coming. Though the church grew rapidly, it was another sixteen years before Walter launched a second location. Like the original campus, this one was met with much fanfare and an instant, committed core group. Over a half century later, the movement that Walter began is a global endeavor. In addition to half a dozen campuses around the world, the church has spawned a recording label, a radio network, and even a movie studio. Every single day of the year, people visit from all over the world to see exactly how Walter's team delivers a consistent experience and makes it seem so effortless.

By now you're in one of two camps: you've either caught on to the story, or you're curiously searching the Internet for more information on this "Pastor Walter" you've never heard of. This is probably a good time to tell you that I haven't been entirely honest in telling this story. In fact, I took a lot of dramatic license with Walter's story, because Walter himself had a flair for the dramatic, for fanciful stories, and for inventing new worlds altogether. What if I told you that Walter didn't start a church, but a theme park? And that he wasn't a gifted pastor, but a master entertainer? While you might have never heard of Pastor Walter, surely you know Walter Elias Disney, one of the greatest legends in entertainment history.

If you have been to a Disney park, you know that they give

fastidious attention to the full show that precedes the message. They strive for a cohesive, continuous, contradiction-free experience. From the reservation process that begins months in advance to the shuttle bus back to the airport, from the restrooms that are cleaned every thirty minutes to the magic that awaits around every corner, the Disney team has placed the guest at the center of their universe.

Now, lest you scratch your head over the fact that I quoted Tim Keller and John Piper in chapter 1 and I gave an ordination certificate to Walt Disney in chapter 2,* let me be clear: your church isn't Disney World. Your church shouldn't strive to be Disney World. Neither should you aim for Apple or shoot for Starbucks. Those companies tend to be the go-to places to learn how to generate a passionate, raving-fan client base. And they're the go-to places for a reason: *they are excellent at it.* If we are just discussing the company's product, and that product was of equal quality and price, I would still choose Disney over Six Flags, Apple over Dell, and Starbucks over gas station coffee because the experience is usually superior. I get the sense that these people actually *want* me to show up.

For Walt Disney, the driving force behind his vision was happiness. He wanted happy parents and happy kids walking the streets of his park. That vision of happiness pervaded everything he did. And with that as his goal, he strategically laid out every other part of his vision to get there in the most direct route possible. On that opening day in 1955, he said that Disneyland would be "dedicated to the ideals, the dreams, and the hard facts that have created America . . . with hope that it will be a source of joy and inspiration to all the world."[2]

---

* *Mouse*ter of divinity? Yes? No? Okay, moving along then . . .

A TRUER AND BETTER KINGDOM

You don't need me to tell you that there is an inherent danger in modeling our guest service processes after corporations that peddle coffee, computers, or costumed characters. Those organizations market a "product," one that is consumable, disposable, and temporary. Eventually my Mac needs to be upgraded.* Every couple of weeks, I have to buy more coffee beans. And a day after I return from "the happiest place on earth," the thrill of Space Mountain is replaced with the drudgery of my to-do list. Walt's plan for my happiness has faded into the background as real life takes over.

And that's the magic of American capitalism: we're taught to want more, grab more, buy more, spend more, consume more, need more. Our shiny toys have to be replaced by shinier toys, and our "once-in-a-lifetime experiences" have to get more frequent so that we don't have to settle for just once in a lifetime.

As much as I love Walt Disney World, it doesn't satisfy my soul. No matter my devotion to Apple, their products don't give meaning to my life. We weren't meant to find rest in the relentless pursuit of an experience. We can't. It has never worked for me. It has never worked for you. And it will not work for the people we are trying to reach. Our desire for more points to that "God-shaped vacuum" that philosopher Blaise Pascal talked about.

But as we downplay the American pursuit of more, we shouldn't be misled: our churches are marketing *something*. And don't let the term *marketing* throw you. Whatever you call it—proclaiming a message, persuading people, displaying Jesus—your goal is to see people embrace something—some*one*—they don't currently know. Maybe your church really is getting by on an experience. Perhaps

---

* Every sixteen days, according to the Reckless Spender Gadget Geek that lives in my heart.

you truly are a resource for the practical, tangible needs of your community. It could be that you're the current spiritual hot spot in town, but unless your driving vision is centered on the gospel, you'll leave your guests empty and yourself exhausted.

Shortly after Jesus's resurrection, he met with his eleven remaining disciples on a Galilean mountainside. This was one of the last vision meetings he would hold with the men who were tasked with building his church. Think about the gravity of this meeting: Jesus was launching the very first church plant in history. The expansion of his kingdom hung in the balance. If these eleven didn't execute Plan A, there was no alternative. How would the world hear without someone preaching to them? Regardless of Jesus's sacrifice on the cross and his victory over death, if they clamped down and refused to carry the message, it was all for nothing.

So what did the founding pastor choose to talk about during that meeting? His plans for a capital campaign? A flashy marketing strategy? Did he unveil the organizational chart or lay out ideas for a new sermon series?

No. No. And no. Jesus didn't orient his friends to a plan or a marketing strategy. His vision wasn't about pushing a product, but proclaiming a person. He reminded them, "All authority in heaven and on earth has been given to me. Therefore go and make disciples of all nations, baptizing them in the name of the Father and of the Son and of the Holy Spirit, and teaching them to obey everything I have commanded you. And surely I am with you always, to the very end of the age" (Matthew 28:18–20 NIV).

"All authority has been given to *me*."
"Baptize them in *my* name."
"Teach them to obey *me*."
"*I* am with you."

"I am with you." Think for a moment about the power of that statement. Jesus didn't promise them a corner office, a winning multisite strategy, a viral marketing campaign, or a popular book tour. He promised them himself. And that was enough.

He's enough for us too. He's enough for our churches. And he's enough for our world.

Let me go back to an earlier statement and turn it into a question: What is your church marketing? What is the product you are pushing? It's all too easy to default to the simple answer of "Jesus." After all, we're taught in Sunday school that Jesus is the answer to everything.* But take a hard look at your current ministry paradigm. Are you really pushing people to Jesus? Are you teaching them to depend wholly on him for his righteousness and not their own? Are you preaching a convincing message that the gospel—if true—really does change everything? Or are you simply teaching people to play church, adopt some religion and adapt to culture, to just come in, sit down, get comfortable, let us take care of the hard questions, and you can be on your way?

You see, it's extraordinarily easy to find ourselves on the downhill slide of simply "providing an experience." It's too convenient to channel Paul's "all things to all people" statement, when in reality we're just putting Sunday morning clothes on a Friday night mind-set. If we're not careful, we'll give some religious overtones to Walt's driving vision of happiness and we'll try to attract people to our carefully crafted kingdom, rather than to the eternal one.

Some readers may think that I'm already making their point for them here. Perhaps your internal dialogue is screaming, "We're

---

* Sunday school teacher: "Can anyone tell me what is brown, has a bushy tail, and gathers nuts for the winter?"

Four-year-old: "It sounds like a squirrel to me, but since we're in church, the answer has to be Jesus."

taking ecclesiology and turning it into an experience. It's become all about show and not about salvation!" Let's face it: for at least the second time in as many chapters, you're about twenty seconds away from tossing this book in the trash can and going back to your Puritan commentaries.

But before you do that, let's take your thought process a step further. If you find yourself in a spot where you want to downplay the *experience* of church, then the next temptation could be that the sermon and service should stand alone. The preached word takes center stage at the expense of all other weekend elements. I agree with William Bradshaw, who spoke on behalf of his fellow Puritans when he said, "They hold that the highest and supreme office and authority of the Pastor, is to preach the gospel solemnly and publicly to the Congregation, by interpreting the written word of God, and applying the same by exhortation and reproof unto them. They hold that this was the greatest work that Christ and his apostles did."[3]

I hope we can agree that the message of your church must be different than the message of Disney World. Your goal each day must be to lead people to Jesus, not to market your church. So if your message is eternally different, that should be all that matters, right? If the Holy Spirit is the one who changes hearts, then everything else is simply irrelevant. You don't need a parking team. You don't need a check-in process for kids. You don't need a plan for next steps. You simply need the Holy Spirit.

I believe in the power of the Holy Spirit to awaken the hearts of unbelievers, convict them of their sin, and lead them to salvation. And I believe he can do that with or without us. In John 16:8, 13, Jesus said that the Holy Spirit would "convict the world concerning sin and righteousness and judgment . . . [and] he will guide you into all the truth." I believe that the Spirit can awaken faith in a college student who is reading Romans by herself in her dorm room. I trust that the Spirit can provoke questions in the heart of an Afghani Muslim who has never heard the gospel or met a missionary. When it comes to convicting of sin and pointing to truth, I do not believe we bind the hands of the Holy Spirit if our seating team isn't fully staffed. He's done okay up until this point, and he'll continue to do just fine even if we misspell a lyric on a worship slide.

My point, however, is not to downplay our need for the power of the Spirit. My argument is *for* the power of environment. The two are not mutually exclusive.

Years ago I had a couple of friends who were dating (I'll let them remain anonymous, because two decades later the story still makes me cringe). It was obvious to everyone who knew them that it was just a matter of time until he proposed. And he did propose . . . in the most underwhelming way possible. They were sitting in his car and he asked her to grab something for him out of the glove compartment. When she reached in, she found the ring box. She looked at him in shock, and he said—and I quote—"So how about it?"*

That's it. No get-down-on-one-knee. No carefully staged proposal. Not even an attempt at becoming a YouTube sensation. There wasn't even an actual *proposal*. This guy had spent several months' salary on a beautiful diamond. He was asking the most important woman in his life the most important question of her life, he was giving her a symbol of his promise to love and honor her forever, and yet the experience of the proposal didn't speak much to love and honor. Did the diamond communicate his intent? Yes. By putting it on her finger, did she communicate her acceptance? Uh-huh. The ring sealed the proposal, but the message of the diamond was

---

* You read that right. "So how about it?"

muted by the afterthought of presentation. Their proposal is not the kind of story they would ever tell their grandkids; it's more the type of story that a still-bewildered friend writes about in a book.*

Contrast that with a husband-to-be who cashes in all his chips when he pops the question. He arranges an elaborate date, has his car washed and detailed, and takes his beloved to a lavish restaurant where they gaze lovingly into one another's eyes. Afterward he walks with her arm in arm to a romantic spot with significant meaning for both of them. Friends are hiding in the shadows, snapping pictures and recording the moment for posterity. He has paid for her parents to fly in so they can celebrate with them. She knows something is up because he's nervously sweating bullets, his hands and voice are shaking, and he seems like he might throw up at any moment. (We tend to do that when the message is important.) And when he finally gets down on one knee and gets around to the question, it all makes sense. The expense and planning were worth it because the environment set the stage for the question.

If you're a pastor, ministry leader, or church volunteer, let me ask: if you believe you are proclaiming the most important message in the world, then why would you not try as hard as possible to create a great experience to get people to a great message? Depending on *environment only* makes it all about us. We get excited about our buildings and our service order and our abilities and our bells and whistles, and we downplay the power of the Holy Spirit to work in the lives of people. But to say that we are depending on *Spirit only*, while it appears holy and accurate, can sometimes serve as a cover for our laziness. If you believe the weight of the gospel lies on one man and a pulpit and it all rises and falls on the sermon, then go ahead and open the door and do your thing. But most

---

* In full disclosure, the engagement didn't last, and she eventually ended up marrying someone else whose proposal didn't involve a '94 Dodge glove compartment.

people don't believe that. We know that the gospel is proclaimed in multiple different ways: through spoken word, relational impact, and experiential cues. We believe that God gives spiritual gifts, and some of those gifts are for preaching and some are for hospitality. You need to trust that the Spirit can work *through* you and the gifts he has bestowed on you.

STAGE MESSAGES VERSUS SIDEWALK MESSAGES

I remember the first Disney trip we took as a family. At that time we had three boys ranging in age from four to ten. For months prior to the trip, we had talked it up, watched the promotional DVDs, done our online research, and made plans from the comfort of our kitchen table. Still, there was really no way for my sons to anticipate what was to come.

If you've been to Walt Disney World's Magic Kingdom, you know what I'm talking about. Just the process of getting from your hotel to the park can make your head spin. Usually a shuttle bus is involved, which plays songs from Disney movies and previews the experience of the day ahead. Then a monorail or ferry takes you from the parking lot to the front gates. But you're not there yet: you still have to take the obligatory photo in front of the Mickey landscaping, go through a bag checkpoint, scan your MagicBand, wait for the rope drop, and finally make your way to Main Street USA.

The entire process from your hotel to the Magic Kingdom can easily take well over an hour, but the Imagineers have developed a system that not only makes it *feel* smooth but contributes to the theme that this is the happiest place on earth. The bus drivers, monorail operators, turnstile attendants, ferry captains, and every cast member you meet along the way are preaching one message: *you are going to love what's ahead!*

But it's not just the people who deliver a message. The setting, environment, theming, and cleanliness all contribute to the Disney experience. Theodore Kinni describes it in *Be Our Guest*:

> All organizations, knowingly or unknowingly, build messages to their customers into the settings in which they operate. . . . When setting supports and furthers the story being told, it is sending the right message.
>
> One of the many examples of this can be seen at the entrance to the Magic Kingdom at Walt Disney World. When you arrive at the main gate, you scan your pass and enter the park through the turnstiles. You are now in an outdoor lobby that features phones and restrooms. Once past the lobby, you walk into one of two short tunnels leading into Main Street's Town Square. The tunnels are lined with posters "advertising" the attractions within. As you leave the tunnels, even first thing in the morning, you smell fresh popcorn, which is made in carts placed near the tunnel openings. The experience of entering the park is explicitly designed to remind guests of the experience of entering a movie theater. There is the ticketing, the turnstiles, the lobby, the halls to the screening room lined with posters displaying the coming attractions, and even the popcorn.[4]

Clearly there are some differences here: Disney is selling a product, and in our churches, we're aiming to communicate a message. But the parallels still apply. Think for a moment about the message your guests experience *before* the message. Does the "sermon" they experience outside set them up for what is to come inside? Are the gifts of the preacher complemented or contradicted by the gifts of the volunteers? You can't effectively preach about the extravagant grace of God if your guests have had to work themselves silly to figure out where to park or which door to enter. You can't convince people of the hospitality of the gospel if no one spoke to them. And you can't talk about "going into all the world" if you're not even willing to walk across the room to meet someone new.

We preach plenty of messages from the stage that just don't match what our guests experience on the sidewalk, in the lobby, in the auditorium, and other places on campus. For example:

Onstage: "We serve a God who shows extravagant mercy."
Offstage: "Hey pal, you're sitting in my seat."

Onstage: "Jesus met people right where they were."
Offstage: "Good luck finding your own parking spot."

Onstage: "The ground is level at the foot of the cross."
Offstage: "Maybe you don't realize this, but I'm a charter member, and the way we've always done it is . . ."

Does any of this sound familiar? Do your offstage messages complement or contradict your onstage messages?

Let's say you invite a nonbelieving friend to your church. Maybe it's your coworker four cubicles over who is an agnostic and is going through a divorce. You've been inviting her to church for months, but she's skeptical of church people and organized religion.

Or maybe it's your neighbor who respects you but respectfully disagrees with your brand of spirituality. At best you're the friendly-but-misguided neighborhood Bible thumper.* At worst you're the guy who will trick his kids into joining your cult.

---

* Unless you read your Bible on your electronic device, which makes you an app tapper.

These are people you may have been investing in for years, dripping gospel truth into casual conversation, praying that their hearts will be awakened to their need for Jesus. And finally, after multiple invitations, they decide to attend a church service with you.

So when Sunday comes, you're on high alert. You're seeing what they see, feeling what they feel, and experiencing what they experience. You're processing everything they hear from "Hello" to hellfire and brimstone. And you're picking up on every single detail that could potentially offend them and undo the investment you've made in their life. When one of your unchurched friends shows up at your church, you might find yourself painfully aware of discrepancies from the sidewalk to the stage.

If your guests show up on an average weekend where average things happen, what will they see? What will they think? What will they feel? If they're skeptical or agnostic, they need one excuse—only one—to turn away from your church. What if that one excuse is that they perceive your church as messy, disorganized, and uninviting? What if they think your friends are not friendly? What if your friends come across as *too* friendly?

Peeling paint and a weedy flower bed shouldn't matter, but they do. One rude greeter shouldn't offset the ninety-nine kind ones, but he does. One inattentive kids' worker, one misspelled lyric on a slide, one overeager membership sales pitch—all of those things speak. And any one of them could be the thing that turns your friend away from your church and away from the gospel.

Now to be clear: that doesn't mean that we are taking the full mantle of life change on ourselves. When we rely on the Holy Spirit to change hearts, it frees us from the failures of our environment. One inconsistent experience or one off-kilter greeter doesn't cause the kingdom to implode. We don't want environments to fail, but when they do, it doesn't diminish the ability of the Spirit to change someone's life. We don't aim for mediocrity, but if we occasionally hit it, the power of the Spirit can still overcome our lack of excellence. The message of hope from the pulpit is far more important than the perfectly brewed cup of coffee from the lobby cafe.

So we have to ask the hard questions about the sidewalk messages at our church. While it may be true that your pastor's sermon is the crowning moment of the weekend experience, it's not the first moment. And the discrepancies our guests see may more than offset the sermon they hear. We have to poke around on every offstage detail and ask, *"Does this add to or take away from the message of the gospel?"* We have to make sure that the message before and after the message is consistent, complementary, and coherent.

Before we move to the next section, I want to offer a word of caution: if you're a part of a smaller church with little or no staff, a small budget, and a nonexistent volunteer team, don't get discouraged at this point. Whether your weekend attendance is fifty or five thousand, my challenge is *start where you are.* The people around us are at the center point of God's mission for our churches, regardless of size. Take what God has given you and trust him to multiply it for his kingdom. Biblical hospitality doesn't need a spot on the staff organizational chart or a line in the annual budget to thrive. Simply take God's kindness toward you and begin translating that into the lives of others.

So with that in mind, let's walk through the weekend experience of our guests.

THINKING OUTSIDE IN

A lot of our churches think inside out: we start with the usually correct assumption that what happens in the auditorium or sanctuary is of the utmost importance. We spend several hours each week planning the music, the message, and the logistics of a worship service. If the stage is ground zero, then we start with the sermon and work outward.

And while you'll never find me criticizing a pastor who wants to give adequate preparation to presenting the Word of God, that is only one part of the equation. By the time guests hear the sermon, many of them have already made some key decisions about whether this church is a good fit. Church growth experts are nearly unanimous in telling us that first-time guests make a decision to return within the first seven to ten minutes on the property. The intangible "feel" of your church, the visual cues you deliver, and the general mood of the congregation will add to or take away from the main event.

Rather than starting with the sermon and working outward from there, consider an alternative approach. Start where your guests do, and think outside-in. Grade the quality of the message they hear *before* the message. Ask probing questions about your environment.* Pretend you've never been to your church before, and think about what a typical guest experiences when they visit your church on a typical weekend. Give some thought to the categories listed below and the questions that follow. Your answers should point to one overarching question: *Does this detail add to or take away from what we are talking about when we talk about the gospel?* Some of these categories will apply differently depending on your church's size or your denominational affiliation, but the underlying principle will still pertain.

The habits and demographics of your first-time guests. Are they attending with friends or on their own? Are they single, married, married with kids? Are their kids younger or older? Do

---

* I get it: your inner rebel doesn't do probing questions, especially when a book starts bossing you around. Just relax and play along for a moment.

they live in nearby neighborhoods, or have they commuted more than a few miles? Which service are they attending? What time do they arrive? If they're coming for the first time, are they early or late? From which direction are they approaching? Which parking area do they commonly choose? Why?

Signage (exterior). What is the first thing a guest sees that is related to your church? Is there directional signage off campus, signaling that they're getting close? Are there billboards in the area or roadside signs to alert them of your presence in the neighborhood? Is there any temporary signage that helps your campus "pop" on the weekend and draws attention that something special is happening?

People. Are you placing your volunteers "outside in"? Do you have people at the periphery of your property signaling that guests have found the right place? Are your team members waving, smiling, and engaging? Are they marked or outfitted in such a way that it's clear they are affiliated with your church? Are they able to greet your church attendees and random passersby with the same enthusiasm?

Parking. Do you have specific parking areas reserved for your first-time guests? What about for other special groups of people, like your senior adults, people with disabilities and special needs, and parents with young children? Does the directional signage clearly indicate where these areas are located? Do you have a way for guests to self-identify themselves as they approach, such as a sign encouraging them to turn on their hazard lights? Are the parking spots strategically placed so that it's easy to know where to go once they exit their car?

First-time-guest station. Do you have one? Is it visible from the parking area? Is it outside or inside? Do guests encounter it before walking into a busy lobby where the station could easily be missed? Is it staffed with volunteers who are outgoing, knowledgeable, and empathetic to a person's first experience? Do you provide a gift? Do you ask for information? Does the process invite or repel? Does it provide a guest comfort or generate additional anxiety?

Sidewalk and outer entry. Do you have adequate coverage at your exterior doors and around the perimeter of your building? If a guest ignores the signs asking them to turn on their hazards and parks in the general parking area, would someone be there to help them know where to go next? Are volunteers lurking inside the lobby, or are they visible outside the lobby doors?

Auditorium entry. Is it easy to understand which doors to enter? Are there certain doors you consider "off-limits"? Are there doors a guest could enter that would put them in the line of sight of people already seated in the auditorium? Are your volunteers trained to know when doors should remain open and when they should be closed, to minimize distractions inside? Do these volunteers act as advocates *for* guests, or do they feel more like nightclub bouncers?

Auditorium seaters. Do you have a seating plan? Are team members in place to help guide guests to open seating? What happens when the auditorium fills up? Do you have a plan for alternative seating? Do you fill from back to front and from center to aisle? Is there a point in the service when you will no longer seat someone? Are there volunteers to assist someone who has to leave in the middle of the service?

Auditorium greeters. Are there people whose sole task is to create a welcoming atmosphere inside? Do they have areas where they are specifically assigned? Are they talking to those they already know, or are they seeking out new faces? Are they introducing new friends to old friends, helping guests connect as much as possible?

Next steps. What happens after the service? Where does a guest go if they have more questions? Who does a person talk to if they need prayer or want to make a decision? Do you have clear action steps from the sermon? Do you know what you want guests to do as a result of their first visit? How do *they* know what you want for them?

What if the buzz after the service wasn't just about the sermon or the music but about the welcome? What if your guests felt the hospitality of the church that was driven by the grace of Jesus? What if people walked away knowing that you loved them, expected them, and anticipated their return?

WHO ARE YOU HERE FOR?

It doesn't matter how established you are as a church. Maybe you were chartered a couple of centuries ago; maybe you're preparing for your public launch. It doesn't matter how long you've been on the job. Perhaps you're brand-new to this role; perhaps you've been around the block a few times and know all there is to know about guest services. It doesn't matter how you label or brand your church. You can call yourself friendly, intentional, open-minded, welcoming, hospitable, whatever.

None of those things matter to your guests. How long you've been around, how much experience you have, and what you call yourself is largely irrelevant to them. When they show up this weekend, they simply want to know that you anticipated their arrival, you care about their experience, and you want them to return.

I started this chapter with a story about one of the world's greatest entertainers. Now that we've reached the end, I hope you recognize that my point is not that we should entertain *better*, but that we should joyfully plan for our guests and pay attention to the details they will see. I'm not advocating that you develop a better marketing strategy, but that you recognize that the onstage message you proclaim should be compelling and free of offstage contradictions. And finally, I'm not even suggesting that you flawlessly execute all of this chapter's suggestions by this Sunday. No, simply *start where you are*, be faithful to the biblical call to hospitality, and trust that God will bring the increase.

Take a moment and think ahead to the upcoming weekend. Someone will show up on your campus for the very first time. Do you see them? Do you care about them? Have you planned for them?

He's the guy in his twenties with piercings and tats. He sticks out from the crowd. You see his far-off stare and his apparent desire to disengage from everyone. But his mama sees a wayward son she's been praying for since he left high school and walked away from the faith.

She's the woman in her thirties wearing a wedding band but with no husband in sight. You see her struggling to get three children out of the minivan and wrangle them to the kids' area. What you don't see is that her marriage is on the rocks and she's making a last-ditch effort to find hope and a reason to cancel the meeting with her attorney later in the week.

He's the professional in his fifties reluctantly following through on an invitation from a coworker. He's an uncomfortable man in an even more uncomfortable suit. What you don't see is the turmoil in his spirit. For all of his success, he's empty. He has searched for peace by climbing the corporate ladder, only to discover it didn't satisfy.

She's the silver-haired woman in her seventies timidly emerging from her car. Her husband is gone, her kids live far away, and she feels more alone than ever. Church has always been a seasonal event, something she does at Easter and Christmas. But she's desperate for community, searching for relationships, looking for meaning.

This Sunday, one or all of these people will walk through your doors. Do you see them? Do you care about them? Have you planned for them? While it's business as usual for most of your congregation, this is the first Sunday for these guests. Their first ten minutes will make or break their desire to return. Their first exposure to your people will either affirm or transform their notions of organized religion. The implicit messages they experience on the sidewalk will impact the explicit message they hear in the sermon. Their comfort level will impact their ability to truly hear the gospel.

Every Sunday is somebody's first Sunday. If your sermon starts in the parking lot, what are you really preaching?

→ CHAPTER 3

When Hospitality Meets Hostility

The salt of the earth does not mock rotting meat.
JOHN PIPER

I first met my friend Tommy across a folding table at a Mother's Day luncheon. My family and I were still relatively new to the church, and we'd been graciously adopted into the fold of one of the clans within the congregation. The Swains were your typical southern family: hospitable, inviting, always had room for guests at the dinner table, and always—*always*—extended an invitation to those who didn't have their own extended family in town. Tommy was the brother of the family patriarch. He was in his early sixties, and how we happened to sit by each other or what we talked about, I don't remember. But I do remember his easygoing nature, his quick wit, and the ear-splitting, gut-busting laughter that punctuated our conversation every few minutes.

In the coming months, we were invited back for more family gatherings: Father's Day, Fourth of July, Labor Day. If there was a reason to celebrate, the Swains were going to break out the casserole dishes and we were going to eat. I looked forward to those meals almost as much as the conversations. As time went on, I realized there was a side to Tommy's story I didn't know. While his wife,

Joan, was extremely active in our church and taught my oldest son on Sunday mornings, I rarely saw Tommy. Actually, I *never* saw Tommy. He would surface at family meals, but he never darkened the door of the church.

I eventually learned the backstory: after Tommy and Joan had been married for twenty-three years, he left. Her devotion to Jesus didn't mesh with his disdain for religion, and he couldn't understand his wife's fervor for her Lord or her passion for her church. So he simply left.

Fast-forward a couple of decades. Tommy and Joan had been separated for that entire time. They lived completely separate lives except for holidays and special events. As it turns out, the times when I saw him were as frequent as the times his wife and sons saw him. During their twenty-year separation, Joan never gave up praying for him and others in her family. Over the years, Tommy's sister-in-law became a believer. Then her husband (Tommy's brother) followed suit. Tommy's kids started attending church. Also at that folding table for our special-occasion meals was a longtime friend of Tommy's named Carl Scott. Carl is a spiritual giant in our church who befriended, prayed for, and shared the gospel with Tommy as much if not more than his family.

Still, Tommy wanted nothing to do with Christianity. A "personal relationship" with Jesus was fine for others, but it made no sense to him. All the prayers and invitations and conversations in the world weren't making a dent in walls he had built around his soul. Even though Tommy had a quick smile, he would shut down the conversation in a second if it turned to matters of faith. He had no tolerance for people who tried to push Jesus on him.

There are many reasons why people like Tommy don't like the church. Some have been genuinely hurt by a religious leader or an earlier church experience. Some view church people as pie-in-the-sky idealists who have embraced an invisible deity who may or may not exist. Some are simply angry toward the *idea* of church, church people, organized religion—you name it. Whatever their reason or whatever their background, they want as much distance between themselves and the church down the street as possible.

I SEE ANGRY PEOPLE

Quiz the average unchurched person about why they're unchurched, and you'll get a myriad of answers: "The church is irrelevant." "I don't like organized religion." "Church is something my grand-parents did." "I don't think there's just one way to heaven." "The church is full of hypocrites." "Those covered-dish suppers are a petri dish for a gastrointestinal train wreck."*

And nestled among all of the rational and irrational excuses, you might find a common metanarrative: *"I just don't like church people."*

Sadly, our churches are home to some bitter, angry people. Some people view their pews as a refuge from the heathens outside. Some church members can't generate an ounce of compassion for those who don't yet know Jesus. And whether or not it's true of *all* of us, we can't deny that it's true of *some* of us. And that *some* is what *many* of our unchurched friends think about when they think about the church.

But before we paint those on the inside with too broad of a brushstroke,† we can't ignore those on the outside. I know at least as many mean unchurched people as I do mean churched people.

---

* I've never actually heard that as an excuse, but you know it's true. Unrefrigerated potato salad is what killed the dinosaurs.

† I know, I know: here we go with the broad brushstrokes again.

While it's true that many in the outside world view the church as intolerant and judgmental, by the very nature of that mind-set they are in fact being intolerant and judgmental. The reality is that not-so-nice, far-from-charitable people are everywhere, and your church membership status (or lack thereof) doesn't automatically make you a bastion of hospitality to all of mankind.

But here's the difference: the church is called to hospitality. It's commanded and demanded of us. The gospel sets the bar high here. Starting in the Old Testament with God's instruction to the Israelites to provide for sojourners,[1] continuing in the New Testament with Jesus's regular demonstrations of grace to outsiders,[2] and extending to the modern church with the exhortations of the Epistles,[3] hospitality is woven throughout the pages of Scripture. We can no more slide past the call to hospitality than we can skim over the Great Commission or skimp on the pursuit of holiness.

Hospitality is a fairly generic term. While you might recognize when hospitality is absent, it's not always easy to know when it's present. Does it mean you have a welcome table in your lobby? Is it training and implementing a guest services team? Is it making sure that you always invite a nonfamily member to Christmas dinner? Perhaps a better—if not interchangeable—term for hospitality is *kindness*. We intuitively know when people are being kind; kindness has a way of standing out. We can all point to instances and evidences of kind people who have crossed our paths. Those are the stories we talk about, replay, and remember.

One more caveat: since this is primarily a book about serving guests who either have shown up or will potentially show up at your church on the weekend, I'll narrow the focus of hospitality somewhat through that lens. But know that the impetus for hospitality doesn't stop at the church walls, and it doesn't just extend to those who come to you. If people are the mission, then New Testament hospitality and kindness should be every bit as present in our homes as in our churches, and in our office cubicles as in our Sunday school classes. The mark of hospitable grace should surround us at the grocery store and coffee shop, and in the DMV line.*

But even when hospitality is demanded of us, it doesn't necessarily mean that those around us will reciprocate. In fact, Jesus told his disciples that hostility from the world was pretty much a guarantee:

> "You will be hated by all for my name's sake." (Matthew 10:22)
>
> "Blessed are you when people hate you and when they exclude you and revile you and spurn your name as evil, on account of the Son of Man!" (Luke 6:22)
>
> "If the world hates you, know that it has hated me before it hated you. If you were of the world, the world would love you as its own; but because you are not of the world, but I chose you out of the world, therefore the world hates you." (John 15:18–19)

Encouraging, ain't it?

In this chapter we're talking about how the hospitality of the church is sometimes confronted by the hostility of those outside of the church. In the following pages, we'll dig into three types of hostility. These aren't exhaustive by any means. You could triple this list over the course of a Baptist business meeting. When we think of *hostility against the church*, I believe we are thinking of three different things. Viewing these levels of hostility as concentric circles, we'll start on the outside and work our way in.

---

* Yes, even the DMV line. *Especially* the DMV line. (I believe the verse you're wanting to quote here is John 6:60: "This is a hard saying; who can listen to it?")

Hostile toward the gospel. This generally covers the unchurched, the unconvinced, the skeptic, the cynic, and the scoffer. Perhaps you have friends in this category. It certainly describes my friend Tommy. They like you okay, but they think your brand of religion is a little too exclusive for their tastes.

Hostile toward a bad experience. These are the people who were involved in a church once upon a time. It might be the young adult who abandoned the faith as a teenager after a crisis.[*] It could be the middle-aged woman who feels like the church wasn't there for her in a time of need. Maybe it's the guest who came a few times but was ignored. And in extreme cases, it could be people who came out of toxic or even spiritually abusive church backgrounds.

Just generally hostile. This takes care of your inner circle: those who are in church nearly every time the doors are opened, but they're never happy. While they claim to be believers, they show few signs that redemptive grace has taken root in their hearts. They're the rule keepers, the holier-than-thous, the you're-sitting-in-my-seat crowd. They're the ones who elevate the bylaws above the Bible.

Clearly defining which level of hostility is being levied at the church is important. Are we referring to people with little to no understanding of the gospel? People who love Jesus but don't like his bride? Or those who are already inside but act as those with no understanding of mercy? When we know where we're starting, we can have an idea of where we're heading.

We'll cover our first two groups in greater detail in just a few moments. As for the "generally hostile," they get their very own chapter later in the book.[†]

---

[*] Church split, political infighting, or bad potato salad.

[†] We have to. They formed a secret committee and currently hold a majority vote.

WHAT JESUS DOES WITH HOSTILITY

Over the last few years, the gospel-driven market has taken the world by storm. What was assumed or forgotten by churches of a previous generation has been explicitly brought back to the forefronts of our ecclesiastical psyches and our Christian store bookshelves. A quick Google search tells me that I can live a gospel-centered life while I pursue a gospel-centered marriage and raise gospel-centered kids who live in a gospel-centered community based out of our gospel-centered church, which will help them develop a gospel-centered worldview.

It seems that we've gospelized everything: music, speaking, writing, publishing, kids' camps, curriculum, management styles, coffeehouses, and breath mints.* We stick a fish outline on our business card and try to convince people that our pipe-fitting service is holier and better than that of the pagan plumber down the street. We've attempted to apply a redemptive, cross-centric filter to everything that comes across the paths of our churches. Even the subtitle of this book could be viewed as an attempt to ride the coattails of the "gospel-centered" craze. But it's worth noting that in all of the Bible, there is no evidence of gospel-centered hostility.

None.

Hostility toward people doesn't mesh with the message of the gospel.

Look at the stories of angry people in the New Testament. Saul the persecutor, "breathing threats and murder against the disciples of the Lord," was confronted and changed by Jesus on the road to Damascus (Acts 9:1–9). In a fit of fearful rage, Peter hacked off the ear of Malchus, only to be told by Jesus to put away his sword

---

* "Your mouth smells like Sheol. Want a Testamint?"

(John 18:10–11). In his writings Paul lumps anger in with the sins of idolatry, sorcery, gossip, and wrath (2 Corinthians 12:20; Galatians 5:20–21; Colossians 3:8). Scripture constantly exhorts believers to put away anger and to replace it with the fruit of the Spirit (Ephesians 4:31; Colossians 3:8).

Gospel-centered hostility simply does not exist. It cannot. Jesus does not ask us to redeem our anger, to sanitize it, or to gospelize it and make it more palatable to a watching world. No, Jesus crucifies our hostility. He nailed it to the cross with her sister sins of lust, pride, greed, and gluttony. There is no redemption for hostility, there is only death. *Those who belong to Christ Jesus have crucified the flesh with its passions and desires* (Galatians 5:24).

But *how* do they crucify it? Let's be real: this all sounds great from a theological perspective. Doctrinally, we can piece together a really good Sunday sermon about how Christians should be colored by warmth rather than wrath. But when Monday morning hits and our personal kingdoms are threatened, when someone cuts us off in traffic, or when the cable repairman doesn't show up when he said he would, it's far too easy for our sinful anger to climb down off of the cross and retake the throne of our lives.

The Holy Spirit dispenses of our anger with the same method he uses to prune away our other sins: *by showing us something better.* We won't become loving people until we see how much we've been loved. We'll always revert back to selfishness unless we see the selflessness of Jesus. We don't have the power to overcome our natural proclivities toward hostility without a better picture of who God has declared us to be. My pastor says it like this:

> The reason many of us feel like we "can't say no" to temptations [or anger, or wrath, or malice, or . . .] is that God does not have that kind of weight in our hearts. God's authority

must be greater than our desires; His beauty should be more attractive than any lust of the flesh. In other words, the reason we can't say no to temptation is not that our desires for those things are too large; it's because our desire for God is too small.

In order to really say no to the desires of temptation, we need to develop a stronger desire for God. Lesser urges can only be expelled by stronger ones. Puritan Thomas Chalmers called this "the expulsive power of a new affection." Our affections for idols are brought under control only when they are taken captive by a stronger, more enchanting affection.[4]

As believers, we have to look to the grace and kindness of Jesus to know how we can be gracious and kind. We cannot create that kind of niceness on our own. Oh sure, as a southern born and raised, "yes, ma'am" and "no, ma'am," "well bless your heart" kind of guy, I can get by on politeness for quite a while. But Jesus doesn't call us to be "polite." He calls us to demonstrate the radical, nonsensical, scandalous grace of the gospel through the way we treat people and show them biblical hospitality. And he calls us to do that even when we don't *feel* nice, even when we don't *feel* hospitable, and even when we *feel* like people don't deserve it. The love that Jesus demonstrated toward us "while we were still sinners" (Romans 5:8) compels us to turn toward our neighbors with that same love.

If anyone in history had the power to make people do what he wanted, it was Jesus. True, he didn't have an army, but he did have all of the forces of heaven. I would think that if a man could raise the dead and turn water into wine, he could just as easily strike someone dead for failing to toe the line. In his own words, Jesus said that he had the power to call down more than seventy-two thousand angels to prevent his arrest (Matthew 26:53).

Note that the irreligious of the New Testament didn't like Jesus because he was powerful; they liked him because he was likable. Jesus drew people in through dialogue, not debate. He saved his rebukes for the religious but gave grace to the broken. Sinners loved Jesus because Jesus loved sinners. He was invited to parties. Little children clamored to be with him. Those despised by society found solace in him. According to evangelist Jim Henderson, "[Jesus] didn't use power to overcome; he used kindness to overwhelm."[5]

I have to believe that Jesus knew a few good jokes and was a great dinnertime conversationalist. I can't imagine that long nights with the disciples around a campfire consisted only of Scripture memorization contests. I'll bet their talks were highlighted with laughter, delightful conversation, and an occasional practical joke. One of my favorite titles for Jesus is "friend of sinners" (Luke 7:34). While it was meant to be derogatory by his detractors, I find it life-giving. If Jesus was a friend of sinners, that means he's a friend to me. He doesn't hold me at arm's length. He doesn't avoid conversations with me. He makes friendship possible because he sought me while I was still a stranger and brought me into his circle of hospitality.

WHERE HAVE WE GONE WRONG?

Somewhere along the way, we've missed that mark of kindness that made Jesus attractive. We forget that it was true in the days of his ministry, and we forget how true it was in his ministry to us. After all, it was his kindness that led us to repentance, and were it not for the grace of God, we'd have no hope whatsoever.

In chapter 1 I led you through a meditation on the foolish nature of the gospel, and I think it's vital that we meditate on the kindness of Jesus here in chapter 3. Have you ever stopped to ponder the kindness of Christ? Have you spent any time dwelling on the depravity of your preconversion life? I don't mean an endless, regret-filled introspection that drives you to despair, but a soul-stirring, awe-inspiring remembrance of the fact that Jesus came searching for you: hostile, rebellious you. Gospel-hating, self-idolizing you. Hell-bound, purposeless, separated-from-holiness you.

He came for you. Lived for you. Bled for you. Died for you. Was resurrected for you.

We dare not overlook the kindness of Jesus in our lives. When I forget about the trajectory of my life before Jesus, I forget about his kindness, and therefore I'm less kind to others. When I elevate my self-righteousness and downplay the work of his Spirit, I'm judgmental and graceless. Worse, when I forget the mercy of God, I begin to build up the warped view that I can earn my standing with him by perfectly obeying his rules.

As Christians, we have a tendency to naturally drift toward law and away from the gospel. We roll deep in the Ten Commandments and fail to remember John 10:10.* When that happens, our rules become our religion, our lives lose the wonder of grace, and we feverishly apply our legalistic standards to everyone around us. Paul reminded us in Romans 8 that the law cannot succeed in doing what Jesus perfectly accomplished: meeting the righteous requirements of God on behalf of humanity.

If there is a black eye on the face of the modern-day church, it may be that we regularly fail to display the kindness of Jesus. In our attempts to keep ourselves separated from the sins of the world, we've forgotten that we're called to go to the souls of the world. We conveniently remember John 17:16 where Jesus said that his

---

* "The thief comes only to steal and kill and destroy. I came that they may have life and have it abundantly." You might wanna memorize that.

followers "are not of the world," but we quickly forget verse 18: "As you sent me into the world, so I have sent them into the world."

There's a balance in being *in* the world versus *of* the world versus *out* of the world. We often do exactly what Jesus prayed we wouldn't do. We're either too much assimilated to the world or too much afraid or disdainful of the world. In the High Priestly Prayer of John 17, Jesus didn't say "in" the world (that's too passive for the believer) or "out of" the world (that's too overreactive of the believer). He said "into" the world.

What does it mean to be *into*? It means that we are deeply engaged with people who differ radically from us in terms of beliefs. We seek after people with whom we're in over our head, people we love, but not people who seduce us. Christians who live *out* of the world are afraid, and sometimes angry and bitter that their way of life is threatened. Christians who live *in* the world are assimilated and seduced, looking more like culture than like Christ. Christians who understand they've been sent *into* the world are deeply engaged but utterly unattracted to it.*

And when people who live *in* the world come into our churches, our theology of *into* will drive how we treat them. Here's a convicting question that I have to ask myself (maybe you can consider if it convicts you as well): Do the people Jesus loves feel loved by our church? When they show up as broken sinners, do they find grace or judgment? When we find out that the newcomer across the aisle is shacking up with his girlfriend or just got fired for embezzlement or much prefers golf over God, do we run to him or away from him? Hospitality and kindness call us *into* the world and invite the world *into* our circles.

---

* I borrowed this idea from Tim Keller. Or at least the notes from a sermon I preached a few years back indicate that I did. Unfortunately, the citations in that sermon were no better than what you're getting here. Sorry about that, Pastor Tim.

We can get the gospel right and still get our incarnation of that gospel absolutely wrong. How can we take the gospel message and embody it in the way we treat others? Pastor Tony Evans describes this as our theology never affecting our sociology.[6] Let's not be a people who are known for what we're against rather than what we're for. The hospitality of the church can be a corrective to society's perception of Christianity. We have an organizational opportunity to promote and highlight the graciousness of God revealed in the gospel. Church people can outmarch, outshout, outprotest, and outboycott all the opposing voices around us, but at what cost?

We start by remembering Jesus's final words in his prayer: "I made known to them your name, and I will continue to make it known, *that the love with which you have loved me may be in them*, and I in them" (John 17:26, emphasis added). If Christians are going to have any impact on the world around us, we have to start from a posture of love. And that love has to be marked by something that carries a similar importance.

THE MISSING INGREDIENT

Here's a fun experiment: every once in a while, ask yourself the question, "What does it look like for me to love _____?" Fill in that blank however you'd like: "my spouse," "my kids," "my hard-partying coworker," "my foul-mouthed neighbor," "the unrepentant sinner," "the high-maintenance church guest," "the Starbucks barista who said 'Happy Holidays' instead of 'Merry Christmas.'"

Only when we ask practical questions can we find practical answers. If your church has a bad name in your community, perhaps you can start by asking what it would look like to love your particular community. Do you do that with a door-to-door evangelistic campaign at 8:00 on a Saturday morning? Probably not. Can you accomplish it with a PR blitz that takes over every billboard in the metro area? That might push your agenda, but it doesn't necessarily promote love. Should you dispense with scriptural exhortations and just let people do what feels good? That could make you popular, but from eternity's standpoint, it isn't really loving.

The balance that Paul calls us to is speaking truth with love (Ephesians 4:15). Truth *and* love. Grace *and* truth. Ethicist Russell Moore calls it "convictional kindness." But we can only strike that grace-truth balance if we share truth with a measure of humility. As Christians, we must remember that we have not yet mastered the art of holiness, and we shouldn't be surprised when non-Christians aren't as holy as we want them to be.

Humility is often the missing ingredient in our message. A strong dose of humility in our rhetoric, our politics, our theology, and our outreach could change an outsider's perception of so-called intolerant, judgmental, and hateful Christians. We should heed the words of John Newton, who warned that the church of his day had lost as much in warmth as it had gained in light.[7]

We should seek to be the kind of churches of which our guests and neighbors will say, "I don't agree with everything those people teach, but I can't argue with how I was treated." We should be the kind of people who hold a biblical view of marriage but make our homosexual friends feel loved. We should preach the exclusivity of Jesus but make our pluralistic friends take notice of our kindness. We should love those still outside of the faith because we remember clearly that we were once outside as well.

Lawrence and Josh are church planters in our city. From the beginning, they prayed for a congregation that would be a microcosm of our very culturally diverse community. At the time of this writing, Waypoint Church has about 130 people gathering each Sunday, with a staggering *twenty-one* nations represented. Twenty-one!

One of those congregants is a devout Muslim immigrant whom I'll call Talib. The people of Waypoint have gone out of their way to love and serve Talib's family. They've thrown birthday parties for his kids, provided transportation to doctor and dentist visits, and helped his family navigate life in America. On one recent Sunday, Talib was sitting with his family in church, listening to Lawrence speak from John 14:6, where Jesus claims, "I am the way, and the truth, and the life. No one comes to the Father except through me."

As you can imagine, that exclusive bid for truth—especially from one of the lesser prophets, according to the Qur'an—got the attention of Talib the Muslim. In the middle of the sermon, he stood up and marched up the center aisle toward the back of the room, where he saw his friend Josh, the associate pastor. He asked Josh to walk with him to the lobby, where he confronted him on the message. "Lawrence is saying that Jesus is the only way to heaven," Talib sputtered. "Does he really believe that? Do *you* really believe that?"

Josh paused a moment, thinking about the opportunity that was before him. But before he went into a defense of the passage, he simply said, "Talib, this is a Christian church. It shouldn't come as a surprise that we are talking about the things that Jesus Christ talked about. But let me ask you a question: Why do you, as a devout Muslim, choose to come to a Christian church, anyway?"

To that, Talib stopped, looked at the floor, and then up into Josh's eyes. "Because those people in there have been so good to my family, and when they invite me to your church, I can't say no to them."

That morning, Talib didn't agree with what he was taught, but he couldn't argue with how he was treated.*

---

* Incidentally, Pastor Josh *just so happened* to have lived in a Muslim country for several years, and *just so happened* to speak fluent Arabic, and *just so happened* to be far

Like a growing number of churches, ours partners with organizations within our city to serve our city. Our people have painted public school classrooms, thrown baby showers for unwed mothers, started Bible studies in correctional facilities, and tutored at-risk kids in the inner city. In the decade since those initiatives have started, we've had to be reminded over and over that there is only one savior for our city, and it ain't us. All the paint and diapers and homework help in the world won't convict someone of sin and lead them to righteousness. Likewise, giving to our city doesn't mean that we receive anything from our city. Community service projects don't always result in a measurable attendance spike. What we spend on our neighbors isn't necessarily reciprocated in the following week's offering receipts. And often our acts of kindness are met with skepticism, disdain, apathy, or even outright hostility.

We've had school teachers who would take our free classroom supplies but ban us from volunteering in their classrooms or tutoring their students. We've had business owners who would accept the free platter of bagels but refuse to engage in a conversation. What we've had to learn is that our resources may get us in the door, but only humility and persistent service will lead to a relationship. And many times it is that relationship that causes our neighbors to pursue a greater relationship with Jesus many months or even many years later.

When we serve our neighbors—either those we reach out to or those who come to us—our service must point beyond ourselves. If we are setting up our churches as the answer for all the ills of our community, we're erecting an idol out of our budgets and our talents. But if we humbly, persistently seek practical ways to love

---

more familiar with the Qur'an than your average church planter. So when Josh invited Talib to meet with him once a week to discuss the differences between the Bible and the Muslim holy book, that was another offer Talib couldn't refuse.

those whom God loves, if we make much of the gospel and little of our goods, then we will be able to help people look not to us but to Jesus.

ENTERING INTO THEIR STORY

Earlier I mentioned the three types of hostility that a church commonly experiences. As a reminder, the "generally hostile" within the church get their own coverage in chapter 5.* For now, let's talk about dealing with those who are hostile toward the gospel and those who are hostile because of a bad experience.

Hostile toward the Gospel

I'm not referring here to those who have never heard the gospel or considered a relationship with Jesus. Rather, I'm talking about people like Tommy who have actively considered the claims of the Christ, who understand what his lordship might mean, but who have explicitly rejected it. Whatever the reason—self-sufficiency, love of current lifestyle, or the idea that there will be time or opportunity to receive Christ later—they have simply turned their backs on the abundant life Jesus promises them.

A temptation in the church is to ignore, fearfully avoid, or scornfully look down on the "radically unsaved" among us. We assume that because we know Jesus, that must mean Jesus loves us more than someone who does not know Jesus. Ephesians 2 reminds us that it's just not so. We were dead in our trespasses and sins. We were children of wrath. "But God, being rich in mercy, because of the great love with which he loved us, *even when we were dead in our trespasses*, made us alive together with Christ" (Ephesians 2:4–5, emphasis added).

---

* And if that makes you mad, I'm talkin' to you.

If God loved us when we were dead, then he loves other people when they're dead too.

So we have to remember that just because someone is hostile toward the gospel doesn't mean we have to be hostile toward them. We can be an *into the world* kind of people: finding common points of connection and seeking opportunities to point our lost friends to faith. That's a challenge for many of us because we're so accustomed to the Christian bubble that we've forgotten what it looks like to know people who don't know Jesus.

I went to seminary in what was then a very small town in North Carolina. We had a McDonald's, a Hardee's, and an independently owned bagel shop, the last two of which were within walking distance of the campus. One of my evangelism professors gave an assignment each semester that required us to have a certain number of "spiritual conversations" with people. And routinely, at the end of every single semester, a number of us would be rushing around in a panic, trying to have "Spirit-led" encounters with people we could talk to on the way to class.

For me, that sometimes ended up being the people behind the counter at Hardee's. When I was popping over to get my dollar menu lunch, I'd insert the gospel with all the grace and dexterity of an elephant being launched through a plate glass window:

"Would you like fries with that?"

"YesandbythewaywhatdoyouthinkaboutwhenyouthinkaboutGod?"

It was all very Billy Graham of me. I've often wondered how many times the Hardee's people were invited to accept Jesus during the last week of the semester. The Hardee's staff was our unreached people group, and we were going after them like a bunch of cholesterol-soaked evangelists.

I had the unique gift of turning real people into class projects. Rather than seeing them as someone whom God loved and part of my personal mission, I used them to have a quick conversation so I could check a box and get a better grade. I'm ashamed to admit that in the years that have transpired since seminary, not much has changed. I too often view evangelistic encounters as something I *have* to do rather than something I *get* to do. I'd much rather skip the process of my relationship with them and just help them start a relationship with Jesus.

In their great little book *Jim and Casper Go to Church*, Jim Henderson and Matt Casper remind us that "rather than talking down to people we're trying to influence, we'd be wise to remember that just because they don't have God, it doesn't mean they have no soul."[8] The remedy? We pursue relationships with unbelievers with humility and grace. We follow the lead of the apostle Paul and start where people are. In Acts 17 Paul didn't use the sermon at the Areopagus to talk down to people, beat them over the head with their sin, or ridicule them for their beliefs. No, he used the idolatry of Athens to engage their culture, something he could do because he had spent time getting to know it. Once Paul found a point of agreement and common ground with his listeners, he exposed the logical fallacies in their search, proclaimed to them who God was, and made a beeline for the resurrection. And what was the response of the crowd? Some mocked. Some joined him and believed. And more than a few said, "I will hear you again."[9]

"I will hear you again." That's code for "Let's talk more." By earning the respect of those he was speaking to, Paul earned the right to speak to them again. He didn't gain that by being an evangelical bully. He received permission to pursue a relationship because he figured out what it meant to be "all things to all people" (1 Corinthians 9:22), and he met them right where they were.

When unsaved people show up at your church on the weekend, how do you engage them? Do you subconsciously put a big red

X on their chests and pull out your gospel rifle for a little soul-winning target practice? Do you eye them with suspicion, hoping that the smell of cigarette smoke they brought with them doesn't permeate the upholstery on your pews? Or do you view them as real people with real needs, doubts, fears, and questions about what life with Jesus might look like? Do you gloss over the need for their relationship with *you* and instead try to fast-track them to a relationship with Jesus?

Some studies have shown that the average person has to hear the gospel twelve times before they believe. What if your church represents all twelve of those conversations? Don't discount the power of a relationship with you to move them to a relationship with Jesus. Be humble. Be engaging. Be wise. And be intentional about helping people move from death to life.

Hostile toward a Bad Experience

My friend Georgia grew up as a pastor's kid. She became a believer in middle school. In eighth grade she was baptized at the biggest church in her state. In fact, she doesn't ever remember *not* going to church as a child.

But for many years, she fought same-sex attraction. And that struggle didn't line up with the teachings of her church or the attitudes of her fellow church members. When she finally came out shortly after high school, she was confronted with a less-than-loving response. She was told that homosexuals cannot be saved, that there is a special place in hell for gay people, and that homosexuals were a creation of Satan.

Georgia eventually left the church but never abandoned her relationship with God. She said, "I don't know if there was ever the conscious thought that 'I'm walking away.' I just didn't want to deal with the discomfort I felt from the people. There were times that the image of who God was was different, but I never fell out of love with him. I struggled with the idea of Jesus, and at the worst times I questioned it. But I never questioned whether there was an all-powerful God. There were lots of questions but never doubt."

Those doubts led Georgia into and out of several churches through the years. Some were affirming of her lifestyle, but—according to Georgia—devoid of truth ("I was looking for God, and he wasn't there. No one in that building owned a Bible").

Eventually Georgia stumbled upon an online message. It was a talk our pastor gave at a conference, one where he happened to be talking about how the modern church should engage with those dealing with same-sex attraction. She tensed up, expecting to hear the same arm's length, snide remarks she had been exposed to as a teenager. But that's not what happened. The message "was better than I was used to," Georgia said later. "I still didn't like it, but he was apologizing for what every church says about the topic. He was preaching that homosexuality, according to the Bible, is still a sin. But so are pride and greed and adultery. And I'm used to sermons that tell me 'you're different and you're going to hell and your sin is the biggest sin of all,' but that's not what I got. His message was loving."

Ironically, Georgia started coming to our church and started making her way back to Jesus *because of* that talk. She forwarded a copy of it to many of her friends, telling them that "this is not a gay-affirming church, but if you want biblical truth and you want to really be loved, you need to hear this."

Maybe the story of hurt that your guest is telling isn't as extreme as Georgia's, a story wrapped up in years of hurt and betrayal. Maybe it simply centers around a staff member who didn't follow up with them like they promised. It could be that they couldn't park where they wanted or sit in the seat they had picked out. Whether it's your fault or theirs doesn't matter; whether their complaint seems irrational or not is irrelevant. As a person of humility, you have a responsibility to hear them and help them out. Doing so doesn't just create a better experience for the guest, it displays a demonstration of the gospel.

Criticism is a gift that we receive from our guests. Whether it's criticism of our programming, our processes, or our people, a critic is like a free consultant who can help you see your blind spots and make improvements. And before you write off this section because you don't have any critics, be careful. You may think that because people are not talking negatively about your church, they are not offended by it, but maybe they simply aren't talking about their negative experiences to *you*. Rather than coming back for another visit, they're just voting with their feet.

Restaurateur Danny Meyer refers to responding to our critics as "writing a great last chapter." In his book *Setting the Table*, he says,

> The worst mistake is not to figure out some way to end up in a better place after having made a mistake. . . . Whatever mistake happened, *happened*. And the person on the receiving end will naturally want to tell anyone who's interested all about it. That's to be expected. While we can't erase what happened, we *do* have the power to write one last episode so that at least the story ends the way we want. If we write a great one, we will earn a comeback victory with the guest.[10]

Philippians 2:3 calls us to consider others better than ourselves *through humility*. It is the humility of Jesus that spurs us to be humble toward others. That same chapter reminds us that Jesus, being God, didn't hesitate to take on the form of a servant, take up the towel, and wash his disciples' feet. He calls us to have servants' hearts like his as we reach those both inside and outside our churches.

"I NEED TO HEAR THAT AGAIN"

Remember Tommy? His story didn't end at that folding table. On May 2, twenty years after he left Joan, he called her early in the morning to tell her he was in tremendous pain. He was suffering a heart attack. Joan called an ambulance and rushed to the hospital to be by the side of her estranged husband. When he was discharged a few days later, she insisted that he move back in with her. He was in no shape to be on his own trying to take care of himself.

Joan had an ulterior motive to her invitation, of course. Even though she still loved her husband and wanted to nurse him back to health, being under the same roof meant more exposure to the gospel for Tommy. Every week she would invite him to attend church with her, and every week he would refuse. But Joan's kindness—along with that of men like Tommy's brother Dallas and his longtime friend Carl—began to wear him down. He started showing up at church occasionally. He found out he had more in common with church people than he thought. He discovered some real friendships with real people who really invested in him. And perhaps most important to Tommy, he didn't feel like he was being judged or looked down upon—he felt welcomed.

On a spring Sunday six years later, Tommy attended services with Joan. After the service ended, he looked at her and said, "I need to hear that again."

"You need to hear *what* again?" Joan asked.

"That message. That was for me. I need to hear that one more time."

And so they returned to their seats and sat through a second service. Ninety minutes later, Tommy was sitting in a room talking to one of our decision counselors. And later that afternoon, I had the privilege of baptizing my sixty-seven-year-old friend as he proclaimed his faith in Jesus to everyone who watched.

There are Tommy Swains in your church. There are Tommy Swains all over your city. Do you demonstrate the kind of hospitality and kindness to them that makes them say, "I don't agree with just about anything those people teach, but I certainly can't argue with how they make me feel"? If Christians are a family, then the weekend gathering is our home. We can humbly, winsomely model biblical hospitality in a corporate setting. It's that kind of humble service that will engage people's hostility and lead them to the greatest humble Servant of all.

PART 2

LOOKING IN

Zacchaeus shifted his weight carefully. He wasn't sure how sturdy the branch was, but he needed to get higher, both to see Jesus and to get some blood flowing back into his foot. The crowd had not dissipated—if anything, it had grown even larger—and Jesus was still the center of attention. People on the ground were straining to see him, jostling to be touched by him, holding their babies out to be blessed by him. And Jesus, ever patient, ever loving, ever kind, worked his way through the crowd as both a man on an urgent mission and a man with all the time in the world.

The initial glance took just a moment, and had Zacchaeus not been paying attention, he may have missed it altogether. Jesus had his hand on the shoulder of a widow, and as his gaze went from the woman to her young daughter standing beside her, he made eye contact with the little man perched precariously in the tree. The look on Jesus's face went from one of kindness to one of excitement, as if he were taking notice of a long-lost friend. He broke into a wide smile, excused himself from the widow and her little girl, and began to make his way toward the sycamore as the crowd pressed around him. They were focused on Jesus, but Jesus was focused on Zacchaeus.

Zacchaeus realized that the object of Jesus's attention was . . . *him.* He went from fringe to front row in a matter of seconds, still wondering if the man from Galilee was actually looking at him or if there was another lunatic farther up the same sycamore. But the next word Jesus spoke dispelled any doubts.

"Zacchaeus!"

Me? he wondered.

"Zacchaeus, hurry and come down, for I must stay at your house today!"

A thousand thoughts raced through Zacchaeus's mind: *He's not talking to me. Is he talking to me? Why is he talking to me? He knows my name! Wait . . . how did he know my name? Why does he want to come to my house? He must know who I am . . . what I've done . . . my job . . . my reputation . . . my character . . .* But as quickly as the shock and doubt entered his mind, it was eclipsed by the kind eyes and beaming smile of the carpenter at the foot of the tree. There was no judgment. No looming sense of condemnation. No hatred. It had been so long since Zacchaeus had experienced the absence of those emotions that he wasn't quite sure what to make of it; he just knew he had to respond. He grabbed the trunk of the tree and slid down, partly falling to the ground below, landing in an undignified crouch as his still-asleep foot regained circulation.

Had Zacchaeus not been so focused on Jesus, he would have noticed that the crowd was now focused on him. Jesus hooked his hand under Zacchaeus's armpit and lifted him to a standing position, and the people around him were stunned into silence. Recognition gave way to repulsion as they realized the rotten fruit that Jesus had brought down from the tree. Zacchaeus. *That*

Zacchaeus. The turncoat who'd become a patsy for the Romans. The pompous coward who'd ripped them off. The pathetic loser who had bilked them out of business deals and savings accounts and financial stability and trust in humanity—*that* Zacchaeus was getting first-class treatment from Jesus himself.

As the silence spread to the outskirts of the crowd, a second wave of murmuring soon broke out. Gasps turned to hushed whispers turned to disgusted pronouncements against the little man in the tree, but also the man who'd given him such value. *"What does he want with him?" "What does he see in him?" "Doesn't he know who he is?" "Surely he knows what he's done." "Why would a man like Jesus go to the house of a man like Zacchaeus?" "He just invited himself to eat with a depraved sinner."*

• • •

To this point we've been looking outward. We've talked about the *outward* hospitality that people experience when they attend our churches. We've been asking: "How do we recognize the natural offenses that outsiders bring with them?" and "How do we strategically identify those offenses so that guests are offended by the right things?" We considered the impact of the details a guest encounters from the street to the seat. We looked at how all things seen and unseen either lend themselves to or take away from the sermons we preach. And we gave attention to hospitality as a lost apologetic, looking at the mandate we have to show genuine kindness to those with a broken view of the church and the gospel.

In part 2 we are going to turn inward. If you are a leader, I hope that you've felt some tension as you've read the first few chapters of this book. You know that if you get serious about changing your culture to be more intentional with outsiders, you're going to ruffle the feathers of more than a few insiders. You will have board members and charter members and big givers and committee heads who won't be excited about the paradigm shift. Looking outward disrupts the status quo and introduces discomfort. Looking outward upsets the apple cart and reorganizes priorities. People assume it's a zero-sum equation, that loving outsiders means that some insiders will no longer be loved and cared for. Reaching beyond our walls will always upset what we're comfortable with.

In Luke 19 the focus of Jesus's attention was upsetting to people. Those who stood in amazement when Jesus turned water into wine, who applauded when he took a little boy's lunch and fed the masses, and who marveled when he gave blind men sight and restored dead children to grieving mothers weren't happy now. In those other situations, Jesus did what they liked, and they applauded him for it. Jesus was helping people like *them,* the ones who deserved it. The crowds liked Jesus because they thought he was on their side.

But that day in Jericho, Jesus upset the status quo. He reached out to an *other,* to an enemy. Zacchaeus was not like them. He was not on their side. Sure, the beggar Jesus had healed the day before wasn't like them either. But he was someone clearly in need of help, wholly dependent on the mercy of others. They would willingly give a few coins to him, but Zacchaeus—that cheating tax collector had taken their funds by force! No, he was not one of them; he had betrayed them and willingly sold his soul to the Romans. Now he was padding his pockets with the fruits of their labors. Zacchaeus was despised, rejected, and hated by the people of Jericho. It was fine for everyone else to receive a touch or a word or a blessing from Jesus. But Zacchaeus? He deserved *nothing*.

When we get serious about loving outsiders, we will create no small disturbance for the insiders. When people who are not like us become our mission, it will bring about change in our churches. So

I hope that I've convinced you that loving outsiders is a nonnegotiable. I hope that you've adapted a "no going back" mind-set. But in our quest to care for those whom Jesus is sending through our doors, how do we love and shepherd those who are already in the door? How do we navigate the murky waters of inward discipleship when people question the necessity of outward hospitality? If people are already on the inside, are they still a part of Jesus's mission? That's where we'll turn our attention to next.

→ CHAPTER 4

Beyond Parking Shuttles and Smoke Machines

Close to where I live in Durham, North Carolina, there is a world-famous steak house that has won every award and accolade from just about every foodie-related publication or organization imaginable. From the massive steaks to their exhaustive wine list to their commitment to first-class hospitality, it's the place to go if you want an unforgettable experience and a phenomenal meal.

My wife and I have dined at this restaurant exactly three times in the seventeen years we've lived here. Once we had a gift card, another time we were with a generous friend on his birthday, and once we paid out of pocket. When I say "out of pocket," I mean that in the same way you'd mean when funding a major multi-organ transplant, because with the first-class experience comes a first-class price. Admittedly, our out-of-pocket trip also included other family members—including one particularly hedonistic and meat-loving son who had requested a special sixteenth-birthday meal. That one meal set me back more than a monthly car payment. This is not the place for cheap people like me. I read my menus from right to left and enjoy anything that includes the word *combo* and has to be unwrapped.

But there is one surprise, an unexpected bonus that comes with your meal. This particular restaurant dishes out one of the best complimentary appetizers that will ever traipse across your taste buds. The staff brings you a platter (not a dainty plate that leaves you wanting more, but a *platter*) of house-made crackers, cheese, pickles, and olives. And they refill that platter as many times as you'd like, which for me means several. The crackers melt in your mouth, with just the right amount of salt and crunch. The cheese is smooth and rich and comes in its own individual cheese crock.* The pickles are perfectly sour and make you pucker when you eat them. And the olives are untouched, because olives are gross. (You know it's true.)

And this free bonus leads to the cause of my problem. By the time I've polished off my third helping of the complimentary appetizer platter, I'm quite full. I never want to see another speck of food in my life. I find myself in a self-induced cheese and cracker coma, wishing that the ground would swallow me up. But, alas, it cannot, because my bulk has increased so much.

The irony here is that this restaurant is known the world over for its steaks, and yet I fill up on the crackers and cheese. What they intend as an intro to the main course, I mistake for the main course itself. And by the time the steak arrives, I'm too satisfied to enjoy it.

What does any of this have to do with welcoming guests to your church? If we equate the steak to the gospel message of Jesus, and the cheese and crackers to all of the unnecessary distractions that we're prone to add to it, then I fear that sometimes we detract from the main course by filling people up on things that might be *good* but not *necessary*. And we can inadvertently fill their spiritual bellies with temporary distractions that have no eternal value.

---

* As opposed to the cheese in our house, which comes in its own individual cellophane wrapper and is in a perfect, bread-sized square, just like the cow intended.

This is a book on developing a great guest service ministry within your church, but to do that I'm going to spend most of this chapter telling you why that *cannot* be your focus. It's sort of like a weight-loss book including a coupon for Twinkies, I know.* But here's why. As much as I love serving guests, as much as I believe that churches should do this with excellence, I need to periodically stop and check my motives. Is being hospitable to people our ultimate goal? Or is there something else that drives all that we do, motivating us to serve others in love?

In the Sermon on the Mount, Jesus laid down a challenge for those who followed him: "You are the light of the world. A city set on a hill cannot be hidden. Nor do people light a lamp and put it under a basket, but on a stand, and it gives light to all in the house. In the same way, let your light shine before others" (Matthew 5:14–16). I have to think that there were people in that crowd who struggled with the idea of being a light. Some were Jews-turned-Jesus-followers, who knew that this teacher had changed everything about their lives, but who were trying to reconcile the old covenant they had lived by with the new covenant they were discovering. Sitting beside them were the nonbelievers who knew that *something* had changed among the fishermen and the tax collector and the zealot and the rest of the ragtag bunch who had given up everything to follow Jesus. They had noticed something new shining in their lives but didn't quite know what to make of it.

And in the fringes of that mountainside crowd there must have been at least a few Pharisees, men who had built their lives on a code of righteousness that was often self-exalting rather than God glorifying. They loved nothing more than to let their light shine. They thrived on being held in esteem by the others. They

---

* If you're keeping track, that's the second food illustration in this chapter. It must be lunchtime.

prayed long public prayers with lots of pomp and circumstance to be known, seen, and revered. They held the respect and awe of the common man, who looked to them as spiritual giants.

To them, Jesus's words stung, because while they were accustomed to letting their light shine before others, they didn't yet understand the two little words that followed: "so that." "Let your light shine before others, *so that* they may see your good works *and give glory to your Father who is in heaven*" (Matthew 5:16, emphasis added). When Jesus rolled out those last words to his audience that day, he was clarifying the reason and the motive for all the good deeds he wanted them to do: "Do good works, not so people will think that *you* are good, but so that they can see *my* goodness."

THE BEST GUEST SERVICE POINTS BEYOND GUEST SERVICE

My family and I live in a medium-sized neighborhood with just fewer than three hundred households and two entrances leading in from the main road. Our home is near one of those entrances, so we see a decent amount of traffic pass by. And because of our location, little happens at our house that goes unnoticed by half the people in our neighborhood. Everyone knows when we've left our recycling bin out a day or two longer than necessary. When my yard needs a good mowing, they know it. When I'm teaching my daughter to ride her bike, she might as well get coaching from the dad across the street, because he's clearly noticing my terrible technique and judging me in his heart.

Of course, this isn't a problem for my neighbors fortunate enough to live in a cul-de-sac down the road. There are about a dozen cul-de-sacs in the 'hood, and to those of us on the main thoroughfare, they appear as bastions of peace and tranquility.

Teenagers can start a pickup basketball game on the cul-de-sac because they aren't in anyone's way. Preschoolers can take their training wheels off their tricycles on a cul-de-sac because it's a safer place to ride. In a cul-de-sac, pop-up canopies can pop up on the weekend, coolers can start cooling, grills can start grilling, and neighbors can be neighborly at an impromptu block party. (Perhaps you can tell I really want to live on a cul-de-sac.*)

Life on a cul-de-sac has many great aspects, but most of those are because the cul-de-sac is not a place you pass by on your way to another place. It's *the destination.* Nobody plans to swing through a cul-de-sac when they're taking a road trip. Your GPS won't take you there as a shortcut or a detour. While cul-de-sacs have great benefits, they're not helpful when you want to get somewhere *else.* They're the somewhere you're trying to get to.

I think about this when I think about the church and the reason why we have guest services. As much as I love what I do, my soul often needs to be reminded that guest service isn't a cul-de-sac. It's not a destination for those we serve. Keeping people happy and helping them is great, but those things are a means to something more significant. The hospitality our church demonstrates on the weekend isn't why we gather, it's a part of the journey. It's not the end, but rather a means to an end. It's a *so that.*

Our desire to welcome people and help outsiders become insiders is good. But if our desire stops there, it can be dangerous. We have to be careful that in our aspiration to provide an excellent experience for guests, the bells and whistles in our bag of tricks aren't just smoke and mirrors. We need a solid foundation that underlies and motivates all we do. If we construct a great experience on top of a shaky foundation, it's eventually going to come crashing

---

* Yeah, yeah, I know. "Thou shalt not covet your neighbor's wife, or his male or female servant, or his ox or donkey, or especially his cul-de-sac" (Exodus 20:17, my paraphrase).

down. And so the way we serve and care for our guests has to point to something *beyond* the way we serve and care for our guests.

KNOW WHO YOU ARE

One of the ways we begin to build on a solid foundation that underlies and motivates all we do is by gaining a clear sense of who God has called us to be. One of the temptations when seeking to grow a church is to develop a cafeteria-style approach to our strategy. We try a little of this, a little of that, a whole lot of this other thing, and then we smash it all together on a platter and try to serve it to our community. While this might add some variety, it also leads to confusion. Guests may wonder, out of all of the options you offer on the menu of programs and services, which is the most important. And members and staff are also left confused. Where should budget dollars be allocated? What should a first-time guest embrace as a first step? You need to know who you are so you know what is most important.

In his fantastically titled book *Killing Cockroaches*, Tony Morgan observes that churches grow when they are strategic in their approach to alignment and adaptability. Rather than saying yes to everything that comes down the pike, growing churches routinely say no to lots of things to make sure they're not doing *too* much that distracts them from their primary purpose. The alternative? Ministries that have grown ineffective and outdated are never laid to rest for fear of offending someone within the church. When we try to make everyone happy, we will end up with mediocrity.[1]

Consider the rise of the "contemporary service" in the 1990s. Looking for a way to reach a new generation who didn't like the old-school hymns of their parents and grandparents, a wave of churches decided to segregate worship based on music preferences, and many added an optional worship experience for folks who liked their adoration of the Almighty to have a little beat with it. The problem was that many churches made this shift while leaving the traditional service time intact, adding their contemporary option at the ungodly Sunday morning time of 8:30. That was always a bit odd to me, since the people who wanted to sing "Shine, Jesus, Shine" weren't necessarily the ones who wanted to rise and shine.

Others, rather than separating the services, blended them. A few songs would get guitar backup and a few would get organ accompaniment, which meant that roughly half the congregation was disengaged and grumbling at any one time. Yet churches kept adding options to keep everyone satisfied, even as people were aligning with their preferred worship style, suspecting that at any moment someone was going to invade the auditorium and snatch their pipe organ or make off with their drum set.*

My point is not to revisit the past to battle between hymns and choruses: I love and appreciate both. But a "cafeteria style" approach to alignment never works. To quote Stephen Covey, the most beloved Mormon in Christendom, we have to "begin with the end in mind." You need to know what it is that God has specifically called *your* church to do and then set up a plan and systems that complement that calling.†

I'm going to bet that your church is not the only dog and pony show in town. Other congregations do some things better than you, and your church is known for certain ministries and programs. The evangelical landscape has plenty of room for people who love

---

* *Invasion of the Organ Snatchers* would make a great title of a seventies-era gospel shock tract.

† Don't worry about what the biggest church in your city or the fastest-growing church in your state is doing. God has promised to complete the Great Commission by the work of his Spirit in the local church. If you are a local church, then there are unreached people the Spirit wants to use you to reach. Put that in your church growth pipe and smoke it.

tradition and liturgy as well as those who love subwoofers and Christian rap. And there is room for churches who trend toward diverse worship styles, because there will always be certain crowds and subcultures they will more effectively reach. One church can still pull off a Sunday school program effectively, while the church across the street may have crashed and burned with it and found their sweet spot with a small-group model instead. Whether it's choosing a worship style or a target demographic or a discipleship strategy, we need to remember that these are simply *systems* that flow out of a biblical calling and mission. Even if there are holes that need to be patched, you can usually pick an option and do it well. But you can't aim for everything, because you'll end up hitting nothing.

So what should you do? Discover how God has specifically gifted your church, and work in the strength he's given you. Your pastor might have a laid-back teaching style. Don't put him in a three-piece suit and try to make him go all hellfire and brimstone. The church down the road might have a huge recreational sports program that is actively engaging your city. Maybe you shouldn't try to replicate it. Maybe God is calling you to something else.

"But wait!" you protest. "What about the apostle Paul? Didn't he tell us that we should be all things to all people?" Yes. Yes, he did. But Paul was writing about finding points of commonality with others, not talking about planning a worship service or developing a formal college ministry. When Paul was "reasoning daily" in the synagogue, I'm guessing he didn't put on his dressy robe and necktie for the traditionalists and then go untucked for the contemporary crowd.* No, Paul was specifically, intentionally

---

* I recognize that this illustration breaks down rather quickly when you get into the practical logistics of fashion. For example: How do you untuck a robe? Don't think about it; just go with it.

studying his surrounding culture, looking for areas of understanding that transferred across backgrounds and people groups. He was demonstrating *contextualization*, a tactic learned in Missiology 101. Paul knew that you have to know a culture and use a culture to reach a culture. To take our familiar message and push it out to unfamiliar hearers is simply to ram our beliefs down people's throats. Paul is encouraging us to find ways to identify with our community without changing the identity Jesus has given us.

Tim Keller reminds us,

> Church models are in one sense unavoidable. The spiritual gifts and callings of a congregation's leaders, together with their social context (e.g., university town versus inner-city neighborhood) will necessarily mean every church tends to be naturally better at fulfilling some metaphors and doing some kinds of ministry. Some churches will be better at evangelism, others at teaching and discipleship, others at gathered worship and preaching, others at service to those in need. We know that no one Christian can have all spiritual gifts and carry out all ministries equally well—this is the clear point of 1 Corinthians 12. It can also be argued that no one congregation has all the spiritual gifts (at least not all in proportion) and is therefore unable to do all things equally well. Local churches, just like individual believers, should humbly acknowledge their limitations and recognize that they are just one part of the whole body of Christ in a city, region, or nation.[2]

By now you're probably asking, "What on earth do worship styles and congregational values have to do with reaching guests? Why should it matter if we choose to go in Direction A or Direction

B? Shouldn't we just be focused on doing whatever it takes to get people in the door?"

Well, yes. And no. Outsiders can spot inauthenticity a mile away. If you're working out of an area that God hasn't called you to, it's going to show. When it comes to defining what kind of church you are, not everything that comes down from heaven has your name on it.[3] We need to embrace the natural tension in every church that while our churches should be *open* to everybody, they're not going to be *for* everybody. Steeple-and-stained-glass First United Memorial is going to reach some unbelievers that Tribe (remember: not "Tribe Church," just "Tribe") in the renovated warehouse never will, and that's okay. One of the surprising things I've observed over the years is that there are unchurched twentysomethings who prefer the idea of a "high church" hymn-driven style of music, and unchurched older people who love a good drum beat. You can't always judge a demographic by an assumed musical preference.

First Peter 4:10 reminds us that the gifts we receive are to be used to serve one another as good stewards of "God's varied grace." The grace that God pours out in the lives of individuals and churches is varied and creative. As believers in your church exercise their gifts, they will create a different tapestry of "varied grace" than I might see in my church. Don't ever try to cut and paste God's grace toward another church into your context. He has equipped your congregation with certain believers who have certain gifts that express his varied grace in a beautiful way.[4]

Your strategy for making outsiders insiders will always target and define your responsibility. Here's what I mean. Whether you use style A, B, or C, make sure that your style doesn't set up unnecessary barriers that an outsider has to climb over. If you're going to do Sunday school, then do it well. Just don't allow your classes to become atrophied in their skill in welcoming new people. If you're going to do small groups, then do them well. Just don't allow them to become social gatherings that never crack open a Bible and lose their evangelistic edge.

The mission we adopt and the vision we champion will give us guardrails to keep us aligned and focused. But we have to remember that mission, vision, strategy—whatever buzzword you want to use—are all what we *do*. They are not who we *are*. They are not our main thing. And when we confuse that, we do so to our detriment.

ONLY ONE THING CAN BE YOUR MAIN THING

Simon Sinek paints the picture of an entrepreneur who is seeking counsel at a dinner party. He's looking for the "next big thing" that will move his organization forward. One friend suggests M&M'S. Another tells him that rice milk is the new future. Another swears by celery, and yet another tells him that Oreos are the way to go.[*]

So the entrepreneur heads to the supermarket and grabs M&M'S, rice milk, celery, and Oreos. He simply had to, because successful, accomplished people told him that was the way to go, and he would be a fool not to listen.

And then Sinek adds, "But one thing's for sure: when you're standing in line at the supermarket with all of these items in your arms, your celery, rice milk, Oreos and M&M'S, nobody can see what you believe. What you do is supposed to serve as tangible proof of what you believe, and you bought everything."

If we return to the cafeteria illustration we looked at earlier, this describes where a lot of churches land. We grab a little of this from one church and swipe another idea from that church and rebrand a ministry from another church, and we say that all of

---

[*] Yes, it seems silly that businesspeople would share grocery lists, but Sinek has sold roughly a billion books, so I'll let this one slide.

this, the mishmash of programs and ideas and values, is who our church is. Sinek speaks to that as well:

> What if you knew your WHY before you went to the supermarket? What if your WHY is to do only things that are healthy? To always do the things that are good for your body? You'll get all the same good advice from all the same people, the only difference is, the next time you go to the supermarket, you'll buy only rice milk and celery. Those are the only products that make sense. It's not that the other advice isn't good advice, it's just not good for you. The advice doesn't fit.[5]

The main thing of the church is not M&M'S, rice milk, Oreos, or celery. Neither is it AWANA, small groups, a Sunday morning orchestra, or an outreach to the homeless. Those things are not bad things, and they certainly have their place, but they're not the main thing.

The main thing of the church—our why for existing—should be defined by God's Word. And the primary message of Scripture is Jesus and that Jesus changes everything. Romans 1:16 tells us that the gospel (i.e., the good news about Jesus) is the power of God for salvation. In Matthew 24:14 Jesus said that the gospel of the kingdom would be proclaimed throughout the whole world, and then the end will come. In his message to the elders in Ephesus, Paul stated that he placed no value on his own life, only that he could finish his ministry and testify to the life-changing power of Jesus (Acts 20:24).

The good news that Jesus brought—real forgiveness of our sins and reconciliation with our Creator—does indeed change everything. It changes the way we live, work, and play. And it changes the way we structure our worship services and our annual budgets.

When the gospel is the main thing, it will change everything. It will renovate our curriculum and reengineer our business meetings.

That's why our quest to differentiate ourselves as a church shouldn't involve a reinvention of the wheel. As I described in chapter 1, we should simply strive to plow a trough straight to the gospel. And when we do that, it frees us to discover God's varied grace in our churches and minister out of those strengths. We no longer have to have ministries fighting for attention if all ministries exist to point people to the hope Jesus offers.

We're also free to explore and express a variety of different ministries as a church. The multiple and varied things we do can be tied together by a common purpose and a common goal: to see people's lives radically gutted and rebuilt by the gospel. When we put the gospel first in our focus, we don't have to depend on bells and whistles. We can—as Henry Blackaby famously said—see where God is working and join him there. When we know where God is working, we know that we have permission to start new ministries and the confidence to kill ineffective ones.

IMPRESSING GUESTS OR MAKING DISCIPLES?

Let's revisit the idea of guest service as catalyst. If we are constructing an argument that hospitality serves the greater good of the evangelical church, then we must honestly acknowledge and think critically about a few points. It's very easy to get deep in the weeds of local church ministry—especially the inside-the-walls, weekend worship portion of local church ministry—and miss out on the bigger picture. Pastors and ministry leaders gain a certain measure of comfort if the attendance numbers are growing (or at least holding steady) year after year. When we look out at our congregation on Sunday morning, we tend to gauge our success by how many people are in the pews. If there are more there this week than last week, then all the better.

The problem with this mind-set is that attendance isn't an accurate measure of health. We know this because there are huge churches that are theologically off base. There are congregations that draw crowds every week, but their purpose is more social than sacred, or their doctrine doesn't align with the teachings of Jesus and the Christian church. Having a lot of people at your church is not the same as having a lot of disciples who love Jesus.

Statistics help us conceal this fact. If the year-over-year head count is going up, we assume that we must be doing something right, right? Maybe. Maybe not. Perhaps we're just better at the Sunday morning show than the other guys down the street. Steve Timmis says it this way: "It is still possible to grow a church by offering a better experience than other churches. This is growth, just not gospel growth."[6] If there is a danger inherent in cultivating a "guest mind-set," it is that our focus on guests—even our noble proclamation that *people are the mission*—can sometimes conceal a shallow gospel culture. We lure people into sticking around for a few months before they realize there isn't much beneath the sparkly surface.

HOW TO AVOID TURNING GUEST SERVICES INTO A CUL-DE-SAC

Following are five statements that can help us avoid turning guest services into a cul-de-sac—a dead end for spiritual growth. You can flip these statements around and turn them into questions if you'd like—questions for yourself, your hospitality team, or your church body to think about. You can use them as probes to poke around in your current culture and decide if your weekend exists simply to make people happy or to engage people in a sin-eradicating, disciple-building relationship with Jesus.

1. Width Does Not Equal Depth

Put another way, outreach and evangelism do not equal discipleship. Churches that care about the guest experience often emphasize the need for outreach. If "it's all about the weekend" is a driving value for your ministry, then you are undoubtedly going to put a lot of effort into the weekend services: getting people there, making sure there are no barriers to connection, and getting people back. The stated goal is to encourage those outside the church to attend and experience Christian community in a welcoming and nonthreatening way.

While attendance is good, we can't stop there. Churches need to teach people to share their faith in a winsome, truth-telling, grace-filled way. And we should do so in a way that evangelism is not an *event* (for example, door-to-door visitation on Monday night or sweaty white guy yelling on a street corner), but a *lifestyle* (Jesus and the power of the gospel just naturally drips into conversations without us making them unnecessarily weird). But I'll say it again: outreach and evangelism are not the same thing as discipleship. They might be the starting point of discipleship, but they're not discipleship. Both steps are important: the end goal of evangelism is to gain a new disciple, and a person can't become a disciple without first having the good news communicated to them. We cannot be satisfied with simply getting people in the door. People in the pews are great, but that is a starting point, not a goal. Further, we cannot be satisfied with merely getting guests to return next week. We must recognize that each visit represents a next step toward a relationship with Jesus or a deeper relationship with Jesus. We must come to a point when we challenge people to a commitment and ask the Holy Spirit to convict of sin and lead to repentance.

Donald McGavran is regarded by many as the father of the church growth movement. As a missionary to India in the 1930s and '40s, he noted the necessary tie between evangelism and discipleship. Commenting on the teachings of McGavran, Thom Rainer observes,

[McGavran] lamented that so much activity was taking place in the name of evangelism but that very few disciples were being made. . . . He coined the phrase "church growth" because he saw that the *process* of evangelism, if it is truly effective, must result in the *product* of church growth. In other words, effective evangelism results in fruit-bearing disciples in the local church—church growth. Evangelism that results in "free-floating converts" with no visible commitment to a local church is ineffective evangelism. Effective evangelism is the Great Commission evangelism of Matthew 28:19, evangelism that makes disciples. And disciples are clearly committed followers of Jesus Christ, followers whose commitments are always manifest through the ministry of a local church.[7]

2. We Should Not Choose between "Go and Tell" and "Come and See." Do Both

Much ink has been spilled on the supposed contradiction between bringing guests in and sending evangelists out. It's true that Jesus never told his disciples to "go into all the church." But that doesn't mean that our churches shouldn't strive to host outsiders every single weekend.

If we champion a "Go and tell" mind-set that emphasizes sending people out into the community and the world, then we are catalyzing people to share the good news of Jesus. As people share that good news, some of their friends, coworkers, and neighbors will respond to it. And that response should result in a step toward involvement in the local church. So at some point in the future, every "Go and tell" effort should result in a "Come and see" response. I'll raise a question I asked in chapter 2 once again: What will the unchurched friend we invited to church experience if they show up on an average weekend where average things happen? Will that invitation be negated by the reception they receive from our churched friends?

Andy Stanley refers to the merger of these two approaches as an "invest and invite" strategy. He equips his people to start spiritual conversations with their unchurched friends and then encourages them to extend an invitation to a weekend worship service. He says,

> Believers are responsible for leveraging their relational influence for the sake of the kingdom of God. That's the part they can do that we—the church—can't. . . . They are not responsible for knowing the answers to every question their unbelieving friends may throw their way. But they are responsible for exposing them to an environment where they will be presented with the gospel. Anybody can do that, assuming there is a church close by that is designed with the unchurched in mind.[8]

"Come and see" is sometimes labeled as *attractional*, a word that—when you say it in some circles—garners the kind of outrage you'd expect if you slapped a nun's grandmother. (As a simple definition, *attractional* refers to a method of ministry where churches rely on culturally friendly practices to *attract* guests to the weekend service.) But we must not forget that "attractional" was a key component of the early church. Outsiders in first-century Jerusalem couldn't figure out why the lives of Christians were so radically different, and so they showed up to see for themselves. As one author puts it, "It wasn't only the way believers lived in the community that attracted unbelievers; it was how they conducted their worship services, too. Amazement led to attraction; attraction led to observation; observation led to conversion."[9]

Is what happens during the week important? Yes. Is the weekend important? Yes. We should champion and promote programs and ministries that happen at both times because people will come to faith as a result of both of these efforts. I long for the day when we will see as many people receive Christ in a cubicle as they do at an altar. There should be balance, but to reiterate an earlier point, all of our churches will have particular strengths. Some will be *stronger* in midweek discipleship; others will have a knack for weekend services.

3. We Should Not Choose between Personal and Institutional Hospitality

Here's a good litmus test for the guest-friendly culture at your church: Does everyone make an attempt to speak to a guest, or is that just relegated to an "official" team of greeters? We can build the greatest volunteer team in the world, but if the hellos and handshakes come only from those wearing name tags but not those in the pews, we have failed. We can tout ourselves as friendly all day long, but if we only greet because we're *supposed* to, we are simply deluding ourselves and misleading the people God sends our way.

If you are developing a guest-centric system for welcoming new people in your church, the way you greet people will always have a mechanical component. That's unavoidable. You *should* have a plan for parking, a process for evaluating signage, and priorities assigned to a guest's appropriate next step. There is nothing wrong with having these mechanics. For example, I block out time each day to read my Bible and pray. You can accurately predict within a few minutes when I'll be in my favorite chair in the living room, sipping a cup of coffee and spending time with Jesus. Blocking that time off is habitual. It's an appointment I strive to keep, whether I feel like it or not. And believe me: first thing in the morning, I rarely feel like doing anything except hitting the Snooze button.

But my *mechanical, habitual* processes can lead to *organic* change. Often, in the course of that time I've set aside, I will garner a new insight about who God is, a fresh conviction over sin in my life, or a different way of looking at a particular passage. And that's not mechanical, it's all very organic: it's something the Holy Spirit is effecting inside of me. But that organic change might never take place if I hadn't hardwired that time into my schedule.

The process works the same way when we "program" a hospitality ethos in our churches: establishing programs and practices is fine, and there's nothing wrong with doing this. But you need to avoid letting the mechanical replace the organic. And you need to regularly evaluate if your programs and processes are truly helping people or if you are just going through the motions. A volunteer might do a great job of greeting guests at the front door during the early service. But if that volunteer takes off their name tag, walks into the later service to worship with their family, and never speaks to anyone around them, that spirit of hospitality doesn't seem to have penetrated their heart. They've never moved past the mechanical assignment. Similarly, if you or I lead by putting all of the processes in place for the weekend but we never invite an outsider into our homes or lives during the week, then we may have misunderstood the organic nature of Christian hospitality.

Institutional hospitality—the "big picture" systems we install in our weekend experience—can be healthy and life-giving. Having a person who owns the plan and a team that works the plan can encourage faith and help people see the grace of God on display. But if the institution fails to encourage and develop personal habits and desires to show hospitality, then we can't really say that we've loved people well.

4. We Should Weed Out and Replant Cultural Mind-Sets

Effectively making disciples means taking the jackhammer to two dominant worldviews. If you polled people in your church or community, 99.9 percent of them would be unaware that they hold these views. But they are present, nonetheless, and we must be aware of them if we are going to change them.

Worldview number one primarily affects those *inside* the church, and it's the assumption that the church exists for them—the insiders. And in one sense, that's true: if the church is a body, then it is necessarily a body made up of interrelated parts and those parts exist for the good of the whole. In 1 Corinthians 12 the apostle Paul illustrated this when he said that the hands and feet and eyes and ears and kidneys and toenails of the corporate body are all individually redeemed parts of the whole body.* You can't be a part of the body of Christ if you've not first been redeemed by Christ.

But just because we recognize that the church is interconnected and gathers as a body doesn't mean that unbelievers aren't to be found in our gatherings. Just two chapters later, in 1 Corinthians 14, Paul matter-of-factly assumed that "outsiders or unbelievers" will be present when the church worships and said that the worship of God by believers will lead these unbelievers to experience the conviction of the Spirit. To put it simply, we must always assume that we have

---

* That's right: someone in the body is a toenail. It's probably you. Don't fight it.

outsiders in our midst. As Andy Stanley often says to church leaders: "Assume they're in the room." Many churched people—insiders—fail to remember this, and as a result much of what we do in our weekend services is designed to serve the needs of the church, to keep us comfortable and satisfied. If we want to make disciples out of the unbelievers already among us, we have to retrain our brains. We need to consider the needs of those who don't yet know Jesus.

Worldview number two is commonly held by unbelievers, and it's the flip side of worldview number one. Many unbelievers are convinced that the church isn't for them. Just as believers have subconsciously propagated the idea that church *is* for them, unbelievers carry the bias that church *isn't* for them. And that's a problem because Jesus said so. When he was called to the carpet by self-righteous Pharisees who didn't like the people he was having dinner with, Jesus replied, "Those who are well have no need of a physician, but those who are sick. I have not come to call the righteous but sinners to repentance" (Luke 5:31–32). Jesus came to seek and save those who are lost, far from God, and in need of the help only he can provide.

Here's a question that bears repeating: Do the people who aren't *like* you feel *liked* by you? If someone feels like they don't belong at your church, what are you doing to dispel that feeling? We should strive to make our weekend gatherings warm and welcoming so that people feel drawn into friendship with us—even if they don't yet feel drawn to Jesus. God may use that platform of friendship to point them to the gospel, but the chances are pretty good that they may never know his kindness if they don't first see ours.

5. We Remind Our Teams That Hospitality Is a Catalyst

If you're a leader, knowing what you read in this book won't benefit or change your church if you keep it to yourself. We constantly have to champion the core ideas we're covering in this book, namely, that people are our mission, and that our guest service teams exist to usher those people to the gospel. We need to keep reminding people that though we pour coffee, we are not there primarily to pour coffee. We direct traffic, but we are not traffic cops. We want a smooth, error-free service, but we don't show up so that the weekend service will run more smoothly. No, we do all that we do as a living, breathing example of the grace of God, our small acts of service serving as a witness to God's goodness in the life of an unbeliever.

That's why it's important to push the *vision* for serving guests at every opportunity. That's why you have to remind your volunteers and your congregation that they are more than car parkers or bulletin distributors. Each one of them is there to help people see Jesus more clearly. One of the best ways to push the vision is through stories. As a leader, you need a "story repository" of ten or fifteen great tales that relate volunteer heroics, ministry wins, and life change in action. When you're bringing a new volunteer or a new hire on board, when you're clarifying your mission or correcting mistakes, you need to tell those stories. Stories help people connect the dots between the way the people in your stories served and how Jesus saved. Show how the work they did helped pave the road toward a gospel awakening that a guest experienced.

As others have said many times, vision leaks. A volunteer that catches the vision today may forget it six months from now. You should never assume that everyone on your team is on board with the vision. For that matter, you should never assume that *you* are on board with the vision. I say that because I find that I must constantly remind myself of why I do what I do—and I'm the guy writing this book! The vision is not about making myself or our church look better; it's not to outdo the other congregation down the street; it's to make much of Jesus. Drive that deep as your primary value. It will keep you from drifting off course as you love and serve people. You'll remember who and what your service is for.

KEEP THE MAIN THING ON YOUR BRAIN

You've probably heard the evangelistic story of the lifesaving station. It used to be hot in student ministry preaching circles.[10] According to historical lore, there was a small band of people who lived on a dangerous seacoast where many shipwrecks occurred and many sailors and passengers perished. These people were dedicated to watching their little corner of the sea, guiding ships to the harbor, and rowing out into the unforgiving waters to pluck people from danger and bring them to safety.

As the years went by, some of the lifesaving station charter members decided they needed better headquarters: a place with more comfortable furnishings and better conveniences. The station gradually became a place to hang out rather than a base to send out. A few people still went on the lifesaving missions, but when they returned with dirty, wet, nearly drowned people, those who stayed back at the station complained that the new people were ruining the carpet and disturbing the peaceful environment they had created. Eventually this tension caused a split in the station's leadership, and those who wanted to serve others had to separate from those who wanted to serve themselves. They moved down the coast and started a new station, one that would hold to the original purpose of actually saving lives.

The original lifesaving station still stands. It is well appointed and tastefully decorated, a fortress of rest for those who love comfort and close friendships. The people on the inside have a genuine love for each other and can't wait to get together each week. But every time they walk inside and shut the door, they do so within sight of a shoreline where ships still crash and people still drown.

As often as I have heard that illustration, I still find it helpful because it's all too easy to lose sight of the bigger picture of why we do what we do. When I'm engaged in my day-to-day, weekly responsibilities, I sometimes forget the reason behind the activity. We can polish the experience and look for ways to improve our systems, but in doing so we can also miss the mission.

In this chapter we started with steak dinners and ended with seaside shipwrecks. Those may seem like unrelated ideas, but here's where they converge: we must remember the commission of Jesus, and we must know the role that our particular church plays in his mission. Jesus's Great Commission was to make disciples. The only particulars he gave his followers were to (a) baptize them and (b) teach them to observe everything he commanded. That means there is a tremendous amount of white space *after* the Great Commission and a tremendous amount of room for churches of all shapes, sizes, flavors, and stripes to contextualize their methods to proclaim the message.

Jesus commissioned us to make disciples. He commanded us to preach the gospel and point to the cross. He demonstrated what it means to call sinners to repentance. And when we forget this, our bells and whistles just become smoke and mirrors.

→ CHAPTER 5

When the Older Brother Rears His Head

He heard the music as he crested the hill, but he was in no mood for a party.

It had been a long, exhausting day in the field. He had started work before sunrise and still hadn't accomplished half the things he had hoped to do. That was the way most of his days ended: incomplete and unfulfilling. His life had been that way ever since "the incident." When his little brother left home, his own workload had doubled, the pressure had mounted, and it seemed as if the weight of the family's farm and finances were now on his shoulders alone. His father was no longer much help; he spent most days staring at the horizon, and it seemed that he was more intent on replaying the past than on focusing on the work that was right in front of him.

And so he, as the firstborn son of the family, spent his days working. Toiling. Breaking his back just to eke out a living and to keep the whole farming operation above water. And as he worked, he fumed. He thought back to that day when things blew apart and everything he had known had come crashing down. Oh, he had seen it coming. He knew for years that his brother was not content with his lot in life. He had listened to the irrational rationale, tried to reason with him, tried to intervene. But his efforts were pointless.

His kid brother was going to do what he was going to do, and he didn't care who he hurt in the process.

Their father had never been the same after that day. He no longer found joy in the things that used to give him delight. Every time they sat down for a meal and his father saw the empty chair, every time they gathered for a celebration and noticed the missing voice, it was as if his father had his heart ripped out all over again. He spent most days on the front porch, pacing, walking, staring into the distance, hoping for a glimpse of a familiar figure. But for years there had been nothing. Not a word.

And so, while his father waited around wasting away and wasting time, he had to get the actual work done. Now, at the end of this particular day, he wondered what was happening as he heard the faint strains of instruments. Honestly, he found them a bit annoying. "There's a party while I'm working? Who has the time to plan a party? What reason do we have to celebrate?"

The firstborn son saw a servant exiting the house and motioned him over. "What's going on?" he asked. "What's the meaning of the music? Why are all of these people here?"

The servant broke into a wide smile that covered half his face. "You haven't heard? He has returned! The prodigal is home! Your father has invited the entire village to celebrate with food and wine and dancing!"

The elder son's face fell as bile rose in his throat. He could feel the back of his neck burning, and he wasn't sure if he spoke the words or simply thought them: *You've got to be kidding me. He's back.*

THE OLDER BROTHER AMONG US

Luke 15 is a familiar story that Jesus tells about a wandering son, a redemptive father, and a judgmental brother. But the gospel of Luke isn't the only place you'll find that senior sibling. Our churches are filled with them. Older brothers tend to feel comfortable in the church. They are those who feel more sorrow than joy when a sinner repents and returns. They believe that they've had to earn what they've received from God, and they resent when others—less deserving—try to share in those blessings and benefits. They believe that their mandates are greater than the mission. They pay lip service to God's mercy, which extends just far enough to reach them, but it certainly won't go any farther. There is grace, of course, because no one is perfect. But grace for prodigals? It's unjust, unfair. What did those people ever do to deserve that kind of mercy?

The spirit of the older brother will kill any spirit of hospitality you want to cultivate in your church faster than you can imagine. It's a spirit that circles the wagons, protects the status quo, and guards the inside at the expense of the outside. Its presence is a dangerous cancer that will eat away any grace you try to extend to those who don't know Jesus.

You find the older brother in the nursery worker who refuses to cuddle a baby because "her clothing smells like disgusting cigarette smoke. Those parents should know better."

You see the older brother in the deacon who is all handshakes and smiles with the pastor prior to the service, but in private conversations afterward he threatens, "If you want to keep your job, you'll dial back those evangelistic sermons. We don't want to get too fanatical."

You see the older brother in the lady who confronts the youth pastor about the neighborhood kid who shows up to a midweek Bible study wearing a Budweiser T-shirt. "He has no business coming in dressed like that. He needs to find more respectable clothes or leave."

You see the older brother when the volume of the worship

music is a hotter topic than the outreach to the community. You see him when committees leverage nonsensical rules just to keep their power in check. You see him when people withhold their giving until leadership gives in to their demands. You see him when people say, "We've never done it that way before"; "What does this mean for me?"; "Show me where it says that in the bylaws"; and "You're sitting in my pew."

The older brother is there in your congregation. Maybe a few faces popped into your mind as you read those previous illustrations.* The sad truth is that our churches are rife with older brothers and our pews are full of them.

The spirit of the older brother fills your congregation. And it fills you. And me. So before we point our fingers at others, we need to take a look inside our own hearts.

IN DEFENSE OF THE OLDER BROTHER

Let's pump the brakes a bit. Let's take a step back and ask: How did the older brother become the bad guy in this story? In most of the prodigal son sermons I heard growing up in my church, the clear villain of the story was the prodigal. Sure, he repented in the end. But that was because he had done horrible things that he needed to repent *of*. He had told his father in as many words, "I wish you were already dead." He had taken his portion of the inheritance and left the family in a precarious financial position. He abandoned his responsibilities for a big-city, hard-partying lifestyle. And it was only when he had come to the end of his bank account that his good sense won out and he made his way back home, empty-handed. Up until that point in the story, there wasn't much to admire about him.

---

* You can admit it. This is a safe place.

A few years back I began to notice that something flipped in the interpretation and teaching on Luke 15. Maybe it had always been there and we'd just missed it before or failed to emphasize it—I don't know. Somewhere, somehow, the focus shifted from the prodigal to the older brother. Where we once warned people not to follow the wayward path of the prodigal, now the primary warning tends to be against the judgmental and religious spirit of the older brother. It's as if pastors are pulling people in close and warning them with a cautionary tale: "Don't be like him." Don't follow in the footsteps of the older brother. He's the real bad guy here.

So why has the older brother become so odious in the church today? After all, he was the rule follower, the good son. He was the one who stayed, the one who did the work, the one who obeyed and refused to stray. He easily could have thrown up his hands and thrown in the towel and refused to take on the prodigal's workload, but he stuck it out and got it done. *He did the right thing.*

As a pastor, I've found that I love the older brothers because their good characteristics typically outweigh their bad ones. If you are a pastor or a church staff member, think about this with me: older brothers are always there. You can depend on them to do what is necessary to keep the church going. They are rule followers with a moral compass that guides them to exercise wisdom and restraint. Many older brothers are stakeholders in your congregation. It's their generous, steady giving that helps you meet budget (and, I might add, keeps your paycheck coming). Older brothers serve. They populate your committees, your ministry teams, and your Sunday school classes. They take ownership, rarely waiting to be asked, and frequently step up to take on more. They're the ones who babysit your kids for a date night, who always send you a Christmas card with a nice note, and who often assist you in navigating tricky situations.

I spend time trying to diagnose the disease of the older brother, because for many of the people in our churches the temptations they face are not the temptations of the younger brother—the path of rebellion. Churchgoers tend to avoid the obvious sins in favor of the acceptable ones. And that's true of the guy who lives in my house, drives my car, and stares back at me from my mirror. And what makes us an older brother—the antagonist of the story—is not *what we do* but *the heart with which we do it*.

What turned the older brother into the one opposing the father at the end of the story is his own heart and the underlying attitude behind his actions. He too rejected the generosity and love of the father, wrongly thinking that he deserved his inheritance, that he had earned it. Lurking just beneath the surface of the big brother's life—of *our* lives as well—are three things: a sense of entitlement ("It's mine—I deserve it"), a desire for convenience ("I need this—I won't give it up"), and a maintenance of the status quo ("I want this—I was here first").

A Sense of Entitlement: "It's Mine—I Deserve It"

In an earlier chapter we looked at the problem of the consumer mind-set in the church, that the person who shows up at your church is just looking for what you can do for them. As I said there (and as Mark Waltz eloquently argues in his book *First Impressions*), consumers are *not* our enemy. They're not people we should fear or revile. Consumers are people for whom Christ died. They are the people he came to save. And they are people we should be proud to reach.

So we will use methods that appeal to consumers to establish relationships with them. But we don't want to leave them there. There is a difference between a person who comes to church as a consumer on visit number one and where we want that person to be on visit number one hundred. When a person shows up at your church for the first time and demonstrates a consumer mind-set, my hope is that they will be expected and welcomed. Their consumerism is not necessarily healthy, and over time we hope that they will grow and mature, but it shouldn't shock us. Given where they are in their life's journey, it makes sense.

Contrast that with a guest who has been at your church for six months, a year, or even longer. If they are still trying to answer the question, "What can you do for me?" then their consumerism is not being confronted and challenged appropriately. At some point we need to think about what Jesus meant when he told us to deny ourselves, take up our crosses, and follow after him. If a person attends your church for several years and isn't showing a desire to sacrifice, serve, and love others, then it's reasonable to assume that their spiritual growth is stunted. At some point guests transition from consumers that we're trying to reach to consumers we're trying to tolerate. Now, that same guest constantly reminds you that you're not doing enough, the sermons aren't deep enough, the small group offerings aren't broad enough, the student ministry isn't fun enough, and the church isn't big/small/progressive/conservative/missional/traditional/whatever enough.

We have a problem when our regular attenders are professional consumers. We call them Christ followers, and they show an understanding of salvation, but they have failed to embrace it personally in a way that has humbled them. They know they are sinners in need of God's grace, but that grace rarely flows through them to others. God's grace is a river that keeps flowing beyond us, a light that must be reflected for others to see. If we are not pouring it out into the lives of others, it grows stale and does not bear fruit. That's the condition of the older brother in the church. God's grace is for them but certainly not for those beyond them.

When a consumer first comes to your church, they may say to you, "I like what this church gives me." There's nothing wrong with that. But if we want to disciple them to follow Jesus, we must give them a bigger picture of the church and their place in God's family. We must help them to understand that the mission of the church doesn't terminate on them; it flows through them, drawing them into its outward momentum to reach others. If the consumer-minded guest becomes the focus of our mission, filling seats with immature believers who like the services we provide, then in some sense we've failed them. Our work is to see them become a part of the mission. And we know we've done this when we've helped them take the mercy that they've received and share it with others.

The church is not a social club. And we're not recruiting club members. In some churches, the path of spiritual maturity is learning the layout of the building, graduating from the membership class, and getting personalized tithing envelopes. If you show up long enough, you'll feel like you've gotten your ecclesiastical ticket punched and you've done everything you need to do to be accepted by Jesus and be a part of his church. These things might be convenient mileposts, but they don't signal our arrival at the destination. None of these are signs of spiritual maturity. And they aren't the goal of our ministry.

A Desire for Convenience: "I Need This—I Won't Give It Up"

A second characteristic that we find in the heart of the older brother is a desire for convenience. Most often this comes across as a sense of perceived need. We find this whenever we are tempted to think that *being* served is more important than serving others.

We see this in Scripture when we read about Jesus's displeasure when he visited the temple. Do you remember that story? Meek, mild-mannered Jesus started flipping tables, cracking whips, and running off the money changers. His righteous anger arose from the actions of the temple officials who were sanctioning the needs of the "regulars" and superseding the needs of the newcomers, the outsiders.

To understand this nuance in the story, it's helpful to have some architectural background about the temple. The Jewish temple was divided into various sections. There was the holy of holies, where the high priest would go once a year to intercede on behalf of the nation. Outside of that was an area reserved only for the priests. Beyond that was the Court of the Israelites and then the Court of Women, where any Jewish-born person could come to learn, worship, and make sacrifices.

But there was one additional section of the temple just outside the gates. The Court of Gentiles was an area that God commanded to be built so that those who weren't Jews could observe what was happening on the inside. Low-slung screens allowed these interested non-Jews to see Jewish worship and sacrifice in progress. God designed this area to give all people a glimpse of his desire to reach all nations.*

There was just one problem. The money changers had other plans. They had found a way to profit from the worshipers who were coming to the temple, and they had set up shop in the Court of Women, providing lambs and turtledoves for the convenience of those who had come to sacrifice. But the offerings there went beyond legitimate needs. Shrewd businessmen had set up kiosks that turned the temple into a state fair. You could buy I Survived Herod's Temple T-shirts, pay a few shekels and take your kids to the Presacrifice Petting Zoo, or stop by the ATM and withdraw some money to grab a churro on the way out.†

---

* Think of it as Six Flags Over Israel, except instead of being in the park, you're in the parking lot, and instead of Six Flags, it's Seven Branches on the golden lampstand, and instead of . . . you know what? Never mind. Don't think of it that way at all.

† Well, well, well. Guess whose Six Flags metaphor wasn't so silly after all?

Okay, maybe I'm exaggerating a bit. But there was enough of this moneygrubbing that Jesus grew furious and angry. It wasn't just a matter of taking money or selling things; Jesus was angry because these activities were affecting what those on the outside saw and experienced. My pastor says it like this:

> Typically, when I hear pastors preach on Jesus' words [in Mark 11], I hear them focus on the last part only—how angry Jesus was at those who were using the temple to make money. But don't miss the first part of his statement: "My house was designated to be a house of prayer for the nations." Jesus was angry not only at what they were doing, but also at what they were *obscuring*. They had transformed the only open-access point for the Gentiles into a catalogue of comforts and conveniences for the already saved. Having a place to change money and buy and sell sacrifices so close to the altar was very convenient for believers and served their needs well, but it kept outsiders from being able to see what was going on.[1]

The money changers were providing a service, but they were obscuring the worship of the nations. Those on the outside could not observe the worship of the temple, and the house of prayer for the nations was now a convenience store for the regulars from the neighborhood. And all of this was enough to make the Son of God kick over some furniture and brandish a whip.

We can be guilty of the same thing in our churches today. A desire for convenience can sometimes, even unintentionally, exclude those who have shown up for a glimpse of Jesus. By "convenience" I mean anything that makes life easier for us (the insiders) but difficult for outsiders. We gravitate toward language that we understand, but can outsiders understand it? We rest on traditions that bring us comfort but cause those who are unfamiliar with them to feel embarrassed or confused. If you've ever been a guest in a church where you were asked to stand and introduce yourself or to raise your hand to indicate you're a guest or to remain seated while others tower around you to "make you feel welcome," you know exactly what I mean.*

When we place our convenience over the genuine needs of our guests, or worse, get in the way of their hunger to see and experience God, we've failed them. Worse, we've put our needs before theirs. When the church is about us and our conveniences, we become dull to the calling of God to live on mission and to serve the needs of others.

Maintaining the Status Quo: "I Want This—and I Was Here First"

While entitlement is understandable and convenience can spring from well-meaning innocence, the third motive of the older brother is more sinister. If the heart of a consumer Christian is not redeemed by the gospel, the spirit of the older brother will soon find a home there. Churches that are filled with people like this will often seek to maintain the status quo, no longer asking themselves what is good for the community or what is good for the outsider, but focusing on what is best for *us*.

Maybe you've heard this language creep into your conversations at times. People start referring to the things or ministries of the church with possessive pronouns. It's *my* pew or *my* Sunday school room or *my* coffeepot that resides inside *my* Sunday school room. This mentality may explain the proliferation of brass plaques on stained glass windowsills and memorial benches in the courtyard.

---

* I'm also a fan of shining a spotlight on people and asking them to identify the sin they're currently struggling with. People *love* that.

True story: I once visited a church that had an incredibly small foyer, not much bigger than a modest living room. But the already small space was littered with several easels and what I can only refer to as "memorial poster boards." Some sweet-hearted individual had gathered photos of any church member who had died in the previous thirty years, and with a pair of scissors and a glue stick, filled the lobby with memories of the deceased. What was meant to be a tribute of honor felt more like a macabre museum of death. And as a guest, I wasn't sure if I was going to hear a sermon or a eulogy, and I wasn't too keen on this particular church's track record for keeping people breathing.

Articulating what we *need* can be a slippery slope to demanding what we *want*. And church people are infamous for not wanting anything to change.* It makes sense. As we grow more and more familiar with our surroundings, those surroundings become comfortable and reassuring. They are what we know. And even if there are flaws, they are our flaws. They become precious to us.

Once we get comfortable, it's easy to become controlling, especially if that comfort is threatened in some way. Any deviation from center, any rocking of the boat, is perceived as an attack on our beloved traditions. You might argue that your church is not a *traditional* church. But it is. Every church that has been around longer than six months has already developed traditions, ways of doing things that seem right to them. Our "new methods" are our familiar traditions; we just haven't been doing them long enough to recognize it.

Andy Stanley warns that the gravitational pull of the church is always toward insiders.[2] Churches hold on to a particular style of worship because that's "what the people want," they hold on to

---

* Question: How many Baptists does it take to change a light bulb? Answer: CHANGE?!

ministries that have outlasted their effectiveness because no one is willing to pull the plug and hurt someone's feelings, or they allow decades-old furnishings or resources to stay in place because someone's great-grandmother left both money and stipulations that it be purchased to begin with.

When we grow comfortable with our surroundings, we can start to believe that we've arrived at the promised land. And the pursuit of our own comfort, defending our own turf, takes precedence over the mission. What started out as a convenience has now become a nonnegotiable need. And once we label something a need, we do anything we can to maintain the status quo. Changing old methods, implementing new ones, and making room for outsiders—all of those things can feel very threatening. Recall that in Luke 15, when the younger son returned home, only two characters were upset—the older brother and the fattened calf.[3]

REDEEMING THE OLDER BROTHER

What I love about Jesus's narrative is that he extends the gospel to the older brother too. Jesus doesn't stop at the younger brother. Jesus wanted his hearers to understand that the gospel isn't just necessary for those who run, but for those who stay. It's not just for those who have wicked lifestyles, but for those who have wicked hearts. And if you're keeping score, that covers every single one of us. We all fall into the category of either the younger or older brother. Sometimes we earn both of those labels simultaneously. Regardless of where we fall on the sibling spectrum, the mercy of the Father can still reach us.

Some of you reading this may harbor some resentment against "older brothers" in your congregation. You are frustrated with efforts to maintain the status quo. You feel like the mission of the church is to reach the prodigal, to rescue the outsider and bring him inside, and to throw a huge party every time a wandering sinner comes home. But there are those pesky older brothers who make it difficult. They don't want to fund outreach programs. They complain when "those people" show up. They do everything they can to block progress and to keep business as usual.

Before we jump on the anti-older-brother bandwagon, let's take an honest look in the mirror. I'll bet that if you look closely, you'll catch a glimpse of the older brother from time to time. That's because often *the same things that frustrate us are the things that often characterize us.* If people who judge others frustrate you, you too may have that tendency to stand in judgment of others. If those who want things done *their* way drive you bonkers, it may be that you too want to see things done your way. You too want progress to be defined by the things that bring you comfort and familiarity.

So where do we find redemption for the older brothers in our congregation? How do we reach that "older brother" in our own hearts? The father models four things for us in Luke 15. For the older brother to hear the gospel, we first have to *point him to grace.* Grace serves as the soundtrack for God's Word from Genesis to Revelation. Sometimes it thunders and sometimes it whispers, but it is always present, always underscoring every line on the page. It's our deepest need in life, and I think the reason for the constant refrain of grace is simple: *we forget.*

The older brother had forgotten his need for grace, that everything he had was a gift from his father, and so his dad reminded him, "Son, you are always with me, and *all that is mine is yours*" (Luke 15:31, emphasis added). The farm? It's yours. My house? It belongs to you. The animals, the equipment, the crops, every last blade of grass in every last field—yours. And what's more, my love, my care, and my provision—you have those too. You didn't and couldn't earn any of this; you couldn't buy it; you simply possess it because I love you. And by the way, you are mine too, my own flesh and blood. *Everything I have is fully yours.*

The firstborn son's good behavior didn't make him any more of a son. It was his birth into his family and the love of his father that gave him the right to be called a son. But he had forgotten that truth, and because he forgot it, he pouted over his position and raged over the acceptance of the rebel. When Jesus told this story, one of the clear points he made is that we must be reminded of grace. Every day. Every hour. Every moment.

The late Jerry Bridges wrote often about our need for a "review" of grace. He said that of all the voices we hear each day, we hear our own the loudest. And because we talk to ourselves more than anyone else, we have to be certain that we are preaching the gospel to ourselves every single day:

> To preach the gospel to yourself, then, means that you con-
> tinually face up to your own sinfulness and then flee to Jesus
> through faith in His shed blood and righteous life. . . . You
> can be sure of one thing, though: When you set yourself to
> seriously pursue holiness, you will begin to realize what an
> awful sinner you are. And if you are not firmly rooted in the
> gospel and have not learned to preach it to yourself every day,
> you will soon become discouraged and will slack off in your
> pursuit of holiness.[4]

Older brothers need to be constantly reminded of the two notes of the song of grace. Note one is that we don't deserve it. We couldn't earn it. It's impossible to buy it. We should have a deep awareness of our need, that left to ourselves we are poor, wretched, and blind. But the second note of grace is what makes the song beautiful. It tells us that we fully possess the love, acceptance, and blessing of the Father because we are the beloved children of our Father. We must continually remind ourselves and our fellow believers that God's grace is wide enough and deep enough for others to experience it too. The very thing that we want our guests to receive, the only thing that has the power to change our selfish and rebellious hearts, is God's grace. And we must never forget that we too have received it. We are no more special or deserving of God's mercy and grace than anyone else. We are simply one more beneficiary in a long chronology of the family of God. His grace did not start with us, and it should never end with us.

The second thing we see the father modeling for us in Luke 15 is *giving grace.* Like any component of spiritual growth, this is a process that takes time. Sometimes it takes a *lot* of time, and we never really complete that journey this side of heaven. It's easy to complain about the graceless people in our churches—*those* people over there. We offer a knowing sigh or a resigned shrug when we hear another story of how they are standing in the way of the mission. We commiserate with others on "our side," talking about how much better things would be if they would simply shape up or ship out.

But in the model that the father gives us in Luke 15, we notice that he did not berate his oldest son, nor did he enable him. He didn't punish him for taking an uncharitable view of the returning prodigal, but neither did he allow him to wallow in graceless self-pity. No, he heaped grace upon grace. The same father who received the prodigal also wanted to redeem the petulant. He didn't love one son more than the other, and he knew it might take time for the older son to come around. He recognized the genuine hurt that the younger brother had inflicted. He was fully aware of the additional workload and burden the absent son had created, and that the first family dinner back around the kitchen table might be a bit awkward. But while he recognized that his firstborn wasn't resting in the concept of grace, he refused to let him stay that way.

This concept is very important for those who lead in the ministry of welcoming guests to understand. If you are involved with this ministry, it's probably because you have a heart toward those outside the church and are eager to welcome them in. And complaining about the older brothers you know can come very easily. Blaming your church's slow growth on those whom you perceive as bottlenecks is convenient. Daydreaming about how much better your church could be if you could round up all of the older brothers and send them packing is tempting. But that's not what the father did. His goal was not to kick the older brother out of the family but to change his heart. The father had an inclusive love, one that looked to bring people together in mercy and forgiveness, rather than their holding on to the pain of unforgiveness. Though his younger son betrayed him, he still welcomed the boy back home. An inclusive father makes room at the table for those who strayed *and* those who stayed.

If my first reaction to "older brother syndrome" is to get rid of the older brother, then here's a sobering thought: *that probably makes me an older brother too.** As we saw earlier, our own natural response to the older brothers in our midst often parallels the same exclusionary and divisive attitude we dislike. Excluding is easy. Engaging with vision and recognizing that God's grace applies to everyone in the family is much, much harder.

The third thing we learn from the father is that *older brothers need to be reminded of the vision.* Yes, the father pointed to grace and gave grace, but he also showed his son where that grace leads us.

---

* Ouch.

In verse 32 he exclaims, "It was fitting to celebrate and be glad, for this your brother was dead, and is alive; he was lost, and is found." The firstborn had felt the burn of endless toil for months, possibly years. He had shouldered the full burden of the family farm and kept things afloat after the prodigal's betrayal. Had it not been for him, the family business might have gone bankrupt and the family could have gone hungry. But the older brother was so focused on what was happening on the inside, on life on the farm, that he forgot about what was happening outside.

A farm is not a church, of course, but that's where we need to recognize that we bear additional responsibility as followers of Christ. God has given us a mission to welcome the lost, to seek them out and bring them home. And yet we face a challenge similar to the older brother in our churches. There is always work to do, events to plan, committees to run, and budgets to meet. We can get so consumed with *doing* church that we forget the commission of *being* the church. Jesus didn't call us to be fishers of committees. He didn't tell us to go into all the ladies' quilting circles. The forward momentum of the church won't be built on youth lock-ins or men's golf outings. Those things may all have a purpose, and they may all serve as a means to an end, but they certainly are not the end.

Somewhere along the journey we've lost our way. We get so focused on the immediate demands of the work inside the walls that we forget about the people outside the walls. As we saw earlier, we become a lifesaving station that no longer saves lives. But the unconditional acceptance modeled by the father—to both of his sons—is a reminder that people are the mission and it is fitting to celebrate and to be glad when they return. *It is fitting.* It is appropriate. It's what we *should* do. Those aren't just the words of a father in a parable; they reflect the heart of Jesus toward lost people, those who are far from God. Jesus went to painstaking lengths to make sure his hearers knew that people outside were the focus of those inside.

Jesus loved lost people. He loved spending time with them, talking to them, and leading them back to their Father. In fact, Jesus said that was the whole purpose of his time here on earth. He didn't come for the righteous but for sinners (Mark 2:17). He came to seek and to save the lost (Luke 19:10). He gave his life as a ransom for many (Matthew 20:28). He bore witness to the truth (John 18:37), did the will of his Father (John 6:38), and came to be light (John 12:46) so that we might have abundant life (John 10:10). Jesus wasn't content simply to hang out in the temple for Family Game Night; he wanted to get beyond the walls and add more people to the family.

Sometimes we end up identifying with the older brother, not because we despise or dislike lost people, but because we've lost the sense of urgency for them.[5] The tragic plight of the hell-bound isn't something we think about very often. We forget that we live in a world at war and are engaged in a spiritual battle for the hearts and minds of people. Our attention is drawn to the comfortable, and we forget that we exist for the sake of others, for those who do not yet know God. A heart for evangelism, rooted in a deep awareness of our own need for grace, will always kill the older brother syndrome. If you're seeking the good of the prodigal, there's no time left to sulk.

Finally, even though I'm speculating here, I think a final takeaway from Luke 15 is that the spirit of the older brother is put to death by *constant, gentle pressure over time.* Admittedly, we don't know the end of this story designed by Jesus to communicate a deeper truth. But let's pretend for a moment that the older brother was a real person and his father was really trying to parent both sons at the same time. Knowing what we know of the patient, long-suffering mercy of God, what do you think might have happened after that last verse? Jesus didn't include a rebuttal from the firstborn. The father's charge "It was fitting to celebrate . . ." is among the last words we hear. But what if the older brother had persisted in his older brotherness?

> "Dad, you just don't get it. He's going to rob you blind again."
> "You can still smell the pigsty all over him. Under that nice new robe, he's still filthy."
> "We should at least have him screened for STDs."

Knowing what we know of God and his patient love for the people of Israel over centuries, I have to imagine that despite the firstborn's resistance, his father never stopped seeking him out and engaging him. And here is why I include this: sometimes, we have to face that same tension in our churches. We never cease reaching out and welcoming the outsider. That's our calling and our commission from the lips of Jesus. When ease clashes with evangelism, we err on the side of evangelism. When comfort is disrupted because of "those people," Scripture tells us to disrupt the comfortable.

But that doesn't mean we kick the older brother to the curb. No, the same grace we show to the younger brother is needed by the older. That's why if we make it to step four and the self-righteous still don't get it, we start over at step one. That's what a loving father does. What a loving father does *not* do is call off the mission just because someone doesn't embrace it. The father didn't give up on his oldest son, but he also didn't cancel the party either. The music still played, the neighbors still ate and drank, and the returning rebel still soaked up the royal welcome. Regardless of whether the older brother came into the house, the party still went on. Just because everyone was invited to celebrate didn't mean they were forced to do so.

The message of this book is that *people* are the mission. And "people" means all people. Good people, bad people, saved people, lost people, churched, unchurched, dechurched, hate-the-church, Pharisees and publicans and saints and sinners. Jesus didn't give us an option to decide what *kind* of people we choose to reach. His "all the world" statement in the Great Commission means *all* the world, which means we have as much responsibility to love the curmudgeonly, power-hungry deacon within the church as we should love the atheist, Jesus-scorning neighbor who lives beside the church.

If people are the mission, we must stick to the mission. But how do we keep the mission central to all that we do? By relentlessly, unapologetically, and consistently putting our own agendas to death in pursuit of a greater vision and purpose. That's what we'll talk about in the next chapter.

→ CHAPTER 6

It's Not about You

I'm no stranger to strange conversations. You know what I'm talking about—those one-on-ones where you walk away scratching your head, muttering, "Huh?" and wondering, *What was that all about?* Among the strange conversations I've had, one in particular stands out. It was a real doozy, and I even wondered if I was on a hidden camera reality show. It was, well, *strange*.

We were in the midst of some major decisions about the future of our church. We had hit a huge growth spurt that left us with limited options. We could keep adding weekend services; find a larger, temporary facility; figure out a way to add on to our landlocked facility; or pull out the ultimate trump card—transition the church to a multisite model. It was the proverbial good problem to have, but it was still a problem. We'd been having prayer gatherings, town hall meetings, and discussions both formal and informal to determine the best way forward. And it was after one of these discussions that a church member pulled me to the side and offered a proposal.

"Why don't we just tell 'em we're full?"

I had that deer-in-the-headlights stare for a second. Then I assumed that I had misunderstood him and asked him to repeat himself. Without taking a breath or batting an eyelash, he said again, "We should just tell 'em we're full. There are plenty of other great churches in town. We should let all these new people know that we can't fit anybody else in here and they should find somewhere else to attend."

Now, here is where I pause to tell you that my friend has a great heart for ministry. Lest you picture him as a grouchy old church guy who stands in the front parking lot yelling at neighborhood kids to get off the lawn that his tithe paid for, you should know that he understands the message of the Great Commission and regularly lives it out. And I should point out that he's correct: there *are* plenty of other great churches in our area, and we certainly want to see them grow. My friend may have even had a kingdom mind-set in his suggestion, thinking that we had our hands full and it would be great to see these other churches experience the blessing as well. But that's not what I heard in my head when he shared his idea with me. I heard him telling those outside the church, *"I got in. You didn't. Tough cookies for you."* And it was that inner sense I had—that we never want to be a church that turns people away because there isn't room for them—that bothered me and made the whole conversation . . . strange.

WHEN COMFORT CRUMBLES

My friend is not alone in his thinking. Many people in your congregation may think the very same thing, though they might never come right out and say it the same way. Like my friend, they may even have good intentions when they say it, a hope to see the numerical growth spread to other churches. But there is an inherent danger in this way of thinking too, something we need to guard against in our hearts and in our church communities. It's the ownership mind-set, the me-first way of thinking that says, "This church is mine, not yours. I got the last seat on the bus. You're going to have to find another ride."

Let's be honest. When things are going well, most of us aren't thinking this way. It's during those times of inconvenience and transition, when we're feeling the growing pains, that we start wondering if enough is enough. It's when we need to move from one service to two, or transition to a different style of worship, or move the Sunday school class to the smaller room down the hall to accommodate the growing youth group instead. In these moments, when our comfort crumbles, the grumbling starts. How often have you caught yourself grumbling because your comfort was threatened?

- A full parking lot means we have to arrive earlier or walk farther.
- A new discipleship strategy means we have to give up our Sunday school classroom and join a small group.
- Launching a new campus or a new service means we have to say good-bye to longtime friends.
- An attendance spurt means we have to sit closer to others than we'd like.
- A baby boom means we'll be asked to serve in the nursery.

When the comfort we've created for ourselves begins to give way, we start looking for a loophole, a simple fix to maintain the status quo and keep things normal. Part of that feels natural. When your church experiences change or growth, *you* experience change and growth. Your old friends might find new friends. The way things used to be will no longer be the way things are. So while your love of comfort might be natural, the problem is that it can fly in the face of the grace and inclusivity of the gospel. It negates the message we preach on the weekend. And it can ultimately quench the work of the Spirit in the lives of other people.

FIGHT OR FLIGHT

Among the reasons why people grow disillusioned with their current church and jump to another one, the "loss of comfort" mind-set
is near the top of the list. And in a strange and surprising way,
what originally attracted people to a church may end up repelling
them in the end. Here's an example of what I mean. Imagine that
a family in your community is looking for a new church. They have
a list, even if it is just a collection of "wants" in their head—and
they are working their way down that list to make sure they find
the perfect fit for their family. When they arrive at your church,
they discover that you've pulled out all the stops to make them feel
welcome. You provide easy-access parking with attendants who
deliver a smiling face in the morning. You have plenty of volunteers
posted outside and at each of the doors, accompanied by clear
signage so it's obvious where they need to go. Your facility is clean
and well kept. Your kids' programming is designed in a way that
the children have fun, but they also learn how to dig deeper into
Scripture. Your pastor preaches messages that are challenging yet
relevant. Your band is on point, your small groups are abundant,
and there are plenty of new friends for them to meet. You are well
positioned as a church that attracts people.

Now fast-forward a few years. That new family has settled
in, and the novelty of the attractive church has faded. They've
noticed some flaws. Their teenager no longer gets the one-on-one
attention that the youth pastor gave him those first few months.
Other, newer families are discovering the church, and those other,
newer families are encroaching on the relationships the now older
family has developed. They start feeling restless. They begin to
think about how much they enjoyed church at first and how much
the church has changed since they arrived. "If it weren't for all of

these new people . . ." They never say this thought out loud. They may not even have it fully articulated in their minds. But it's there, looming just below the surface.

I want to be fair here. People have many reasons for becoming uncomfortable with explosive church growth. Sometimes that discomfort is well grounded: church growth can outpace church structure, resulting in an overworked staff, an underresourced budget, and an underserved congregation (see Acts 6 as an example). Sometimes the discomfort is well meaning: longtime church members can assume a parental posture, fretting over things that seem to be happening so fast. And sometimes it's just natural for people to worry that changes in the church could mean they lose their role or ministry identity. The big idea here is not that someone's discomfort is *wrong*. Discomfort *will* come, but the question is, will we force discomfort onto the newcomer, or will we willingly lay down our desires and embrace discomfort for the sake of those on the outside?

Church people experience church growth in different ways. The first way they experience it is as an outsider. If the church has been set up and designed with outsiders in mind, church growth feels great to them. The "new" is for them. The "wow" is to meet their desires. The entire experience serves as a gravitational force, pulling them into the church's orbit. But if growth is geared toward outsiders, some insiders will experience it as a loss or a threat. Eventually your outsiders become insiders. While they've both seen and benefited from the attention they once received, there comes a time when their status may feel threatened by new outsiders coming in.

When people are threatened, they typically adopt a fight-or-flight mentality. And why do church members feel threatened? They adopt a wrong understanding of the church and their place in it. They fail to understand their unique and ongoing place in the church and how it connects with the larger mission of Jesus. And when they fail to connect their place and role with the heart and purpose of Christ, they feel possessive and might be tempted to hop somewhere else where they are treated a little better. They start looking for something new and different that caters to them. Perhaps—like me—you've known a few chronic church hoppers, people who switch from church to church looking for a newer, better experience, but are ultimately left shallow and disconnected from their relationships with others. Instead of fleeing to new surroundings, we have to fight. But not to keep things the way we want them. Our fight is not to maintain the status quo of our comfort; it's to go deeper. We want to grow as a community in the congregation where God has placed us. But how do you get church insiders to grasp their roles and learn to fight for a kingdom greater than their own? How do you help church people push through the "insider" mentality?

Through grace.

WHO ARE WE HERE FOR?

If we want people to grasp their role in the church and their part in the mission of Jesus, we need to start with grace, especially the grace of God as it is most fully revealed to us in the gospel of the life, death, and resurrection of Christ. The thread of grace is woven into every page of Scripture, and seeing that thread helps us understand our place, our guests' place, and the church's place in continuing that thread.[1]

While there are many places we could begin, a good place to start is Genesis 12 when God called Abram out of Haran. His promise to this man was profound: "I will make of you a great nation, and I will bless you and make your name great, so that you will be a blessing. I will bless those who bless you, and him who dishonors you I will curse, and in you all the families of the earth shall be blessed" (Genesis 12:2–3). God's call on Abram's life included a blessing of grace toward all of humanity. Through this one man and his descendants, God promised to bring blessing to the entire world.

Abraham's descendants became known as the people of Israel, and if you know the larger story of Israel told in the Old Testament, you may recall that they are referred to as God's chosen people. His *chosen* people. Just as God *chose* Abraham and promised to bless him, God continued to choose to bless and work through Abraham's descendants. This was their identity. They were part of the in-crowd. In the lunchroom of theological history, they were sitting at the cool kids' table.* But there were hints, even at this point, that God wasn't blessing them for their sake alone. In Leviticus 19 God showed them that his grace to them was not intended only for them: "When a stranger sojourns with you in your land, you shall not do him wrong. You shall treat the stranger who sojourns with you as the native among you, and you shall love him as yourself, for you were strangers in the land of Egypt: I am the Lord your God" (vv. 33–34).

In addition to this word to the people, God gave them particular commands so that they—the insiders—could be a blessing to those still on the outside. The laws about surplus harvest, safe harbor, and observable worship, many of which seem obscure and irrelevant to us today, were intended to train the Israelites to keep their eyes open toward others. We can learn something about the heart of God and his purposes from studying his intentions for his chosen people: God has a heart for outsiders.

---

* Philistines = football team, Psalmists = pep and/or Emo band kids, Priests = chess club.

In chapter 5 I mentioned that when the Jewish temple was built, God told Solomon to include an area in the temple for non-Jews. The Court of Gentiles was intended to be a physical indication of God's desire to draw all people to himself. In Solomon's prayer of dedication for the temple, he reminded both God and God's chosen that the temple wasn't just for those on the inside:

> "Likewise, when a foreigner, who is not of your people Israel, comes from a far country for your name's sake (for they shall hear of your great name and your mighty hand, and of your outstretched arm), when he comes and prays toward this house, hear in heaven your dwelling place and do according to all for which the foreigner calls to you, in order that all the peoples of the earth may know your name and fear you, as do your people Israel, and that they may know that this house that I have built is called by your name." (1 Kings 8:41–43)

This concern for the outsider—the grace of Abraham's blessing for the world—continues into the New Testament. While it's true that the *priority* of Jesus's ministry was to reach the "lost sheep of the house of Israel" (Matthew 10:6), he later expanded that *inclusivity* to the Gentiles.[2] In the Great Commission, Jesus's new mandate was for his Jewish followers to carry the gospel to all nations. At his ascension he encouraged the apostles with the promise of the Holy Spirit, who would empower them to reach Jerusalem, but to go beyond as well to Judea, Samaria, and all the people groups and ethnicities to the ends of the earth (Acts 1:8). Not long after, on the day of Pentecost, both Jews and proselytes (Gentile converts to Judaism) were witnesses to the coming of the Holy Spirit with praises to God in multiple languages, a prophetic sign that God was going global with his purposes (Acts 2:11).

In Acts 10 God wrecked Peter's Jewish world by overturning the Jewish ceremonial laws and Peter's own prejudice against Gentiles in the process.* He then sent Peter to the Gentile God-fearer Cornelius to proclaim the gospel of grace, and Cornelius and his household gladly responded and received the gift of the Holy Spirit. When Peter carried the news of this incident back to the church in Jerusalem, he asked one of the most wonderful questions in Scripture: "If then God gave the same gift to them as he gave to us when we believed in the Lord Jesus Christ, *who was I that I could stand in God's way?*" (Acts 11:17, emphasis added). A few verses later, the persecution of the Jewish church leaders led to further Gentile conversions, and the remainder of Acts is the fulfillment of the promise of chapter 1: the Holy Spirit would use the early church to carry the message of God's grace to every tribe, tongue, and nation.

'TIS GRACE HATH BROUGHT ME SAFE THUS FAR . . .

While there are likely to be exceptions, if you are reading this book, the chances are better than average that you are not Jewish by birth or by heritage. Odds are that you are what the Bible describes as a Gentile. (Me too. Welcome to the club. Insert the secret Gentile handshake here.) And if you're like most Gentile God-fearers, you read the Old Testament and forget that it's not about you. The stories of grace and redemption and pursuit and deliverance are about the people of Israel, not the people of the American Southeast or the Scottish Highlands or the African jungles. We aren't part of those stories.

---

* And giving us bacon. Mmmm . . . bacon.

Unless, perhaps, we are. Just not the way you might think.

One of the leaders in the early church was a man named Paul. A Jew by birth, Paul was originally hostile to Christianity, but after meeting Jesus, he became fully convinced that the blessings of his people were intended for *all* people. In a section of a letter he wrote to the Christians in Rome (Romans 11) he gave a biology and ecclesiology lesson that instructs us on our place in the thread of grace. Genesis 12 gave us the promise of God's global blessing, but Romans 11 gives us the fulfillment of that promise. Paul said that it was the trespass of the Jews—their constant rebellion against God throughout the Old Testament—that led to salvation for the Gentiles through one of the descendants of Abraham. The physical lineage of Abraham prepared the way for the spiritual lineage of Jesus. And every Gentile believer since that time—you, me, and every non-Jew who calls on the name of the Lord—is now grafted into the root of richness, the promises of the God of Israel.

If you skipped that day when they discussed grafting in Biology 101, here's what it means. When something is "grafted in," it involves taking a cutting from a foreign plant and inserting it into a host plant, thereby allowing both to grow into something new. Over the course of a few days or weeks, the tissues from both the original and the inserted plant begin to merge and grow together. The foreign plant benefits from the host plant's root system. It drinks the host's water and depends on the host's nutrients.* Paul said that's what happened with all of us Gentiles. We were grafted into the blessings that were originally given to the Jews. Their grace is our grace. Their redemption is our redemption. Their inclusion is our inclusion. Every promise that was made to Abraham, we can

---

* Ms. Lassiter, if you happen to be reading this, I hope I explained it to your satisfaction. Please don't make me retake the class. We both know that I barely made it through the first time.

rightfully claim as our own because we're now grafted in, a part of the original root.

That's great news for us. But there's also an inherent danger, and it's that our grafting can produce arrogance. Paul warned against this in Romans 11, as well: "They were broken off because of their unbelief, but you stand fast through faith. So do not become proud, but fear" (v. 20). Our inclusion into the promises we did nothing to earn and do not deserve should never mean arrogance or pride, but awe. We didn't do one single thing to deserve this inclusion. God did not *have* to extend his blessing outside the circle of the chosen. In fact, he didn't even have to extend it to the chosen. It is his grace that has brought salvation to both Jew and Gentile alike. 'Tis grace that has brought us safe thus far.

So when we think about grace, we must remember that it's *not* about us. Except that it *is* about us. But it's not *only* about us.

Still confused? Maybe another encouragement from Paul will help. In Romans 12 he wrote,

> For by the grace given to me I say to everyone among you not to think of himself more highly than he ought to think, but to think with sober judgment, each according to the measure of faith that God has assigned. For as in one body we have many members, and the members do not all have the same function, so we, though many, are one body in Christ, and individually members one of another. Having gifts that differ according to the grace given to us, let us use them." (vv. 3–6)

In this passage Paul pulled back the curtain on a Christian phenomenon known as spiritual gifts. If you grew up in the church, you know all about spiritual gifts. Maybe your pastor did a forty-seven-week sermon series on every gift out there from prophecy to prayer. And maybe—like me—you struggled for more than your fair share of years to figure out exactly what your gift was. If you didn't grow up in church, the concept of a spiritual gift might sound spooky or a little bit odd. It immediately generates a host of questions. What is it? How do you get it? Who gives it to you? Do you have it handed over in some sort of ceremony? Do you have to send in box tops from a case of communion wafers? And what if you get a gift you don't want? Can you trade it in?

To put it simply, spiritual gifts are different ways in which the Holy Spirit does God's work through God's people. God does his work through ordinary people empowered by his Holy Spirit, and when those people teach, pray, serve, and bless others in a way that brings glory and attention to God, we call that activity a spiritual gift. And while we can spend years digging into all the lists the Bible gives us, I tend to think we've overcomplicated what the Bible wants us to know about our spiritual gifts. We've taken something Paul wrote and turned it into something with far more steps and hoops than it needs to have. I love these four verses in Romans 12 because before Paul talked about *what* some of the spiritual gifts are, he told us exactly *why* they're important. Because if we don't understand *why* we're given our gifts, we'll never understand *what* they are, and more than that we'll never understand *how* we use them.

In Romans 12 Paul took all of the grace-filled history of the nation of Israel and asked us to gaze at it. But he didn't leave us with an interesting history lesson about the Jewish people. He reminded us that *all* of the Christian life is an exercise in grace. For the first 11 chapters of his letter to the Romans, Paul explained the gospel in great detail: what it is, who it's about, why we need it, and why we can't live without it. But at the beginning of chapter 12, he took a hard right turn, and instead of helping us *learn* theology, he helped us *live* out that theology, to live in light of the implications of the gospel. If the entire gospel hinges on grace, then all of our hope and eternity hinge on receiving and embracing that grace. And so Paul used that word—*grace*—as the key idea in his next statement: "For by the grace given to me I say to everyone among you not to think of himself more highly than he ought to think" (v. 3).

The church in Rome to whom Paul was writing was dealing with some serious unity issues. A body of believers of Jewish heritage there had spent a lifetime observing the rules and regulations of the Old Testament. And there was also a group of Gentiles who had every religious and nonreligious background under the sun, and most adhered to an "anything goes" philosophy of life. And now both Jews and Gentiles had become believers in Jesus, and they were trying to figure out how their past lives intersected with their present faith.

As you might guess, this was a recipe for conflict. Paul knew that some in the church at Rome carried a sense of entitlement. For whatever reason, some Jews felt they were superior to the Gentiles, and some Gentiles felt they had a leg up on the Jews. Individuals in each group were thinking of themselves more highly than they ought to think. After all, as Paul pointed out in his letter, they were all sinners, all standing condemned, and all equally in need of the mercy and grace of God.

While I'm not exactly sure what form the Jewish/Gentile disunity looked like in first-century Rome,* I do know that we have this same "thinking of yourself more highly than you ought to think" phenomenon in our modern local churches. It typically leads to two sinful and divisive patterns that are dangerous for the unity of God's church.

---

* Probably the color of the carpet in the fellowship hall.

THE DANGER OF ENTITLEMENT

Perhaps you are blessed to be part of a growing church with vision where lots of good things are happening. There might be a menu of ministry options, a wide reach into your community, a good amount of influence with community leaders, and a decent-sized budget. All of this is good. But with good things comes the danger of pride. And pride communicates that we think we've earned or are primarily responsible for what we've done. If left unattended, this pride brings us to a point both individually and corporately where we feel as though we *deserve* these things. We develop a sense of entitlement that this is the way things are *supposed* to be. If I'm part of a multisite church, I'm supposed to have a campus in my zip code. I'm supposed to have a choice of a half dozen small groups in my neighborhood, and every one of those groups should be outfitted with nonweirdoes that my wife and I can enjoy hanging out with.* I'm supposed to be able to show up on the weekend and find a close parking spot and a comfortable chair and not be asked to scoot in. The worship leader is supposed to have an appropriate length of hair that I'm comfortable with, and the preacher is supposed to preach messages that are challenging but not *too* challenging. And the HeBrews™ cappuccino bar had better get my foam just right.

Entitlement kills a church. It will bring spiritual death to believers as well. It will kill us when we think we've arrived and the church exists to serve us and cater to our every whim, and we don't ever think about serving others. Jesus knew that he needed to push back against the entitlement mentality. If there's anybody in the history of the world who deserved to be served, it's Jesus. But he modeled a radically countercultural way of living and leading.

---

* Statistically, every small group has to have a weirdo. And if you're looking around your group and can't figure out who it is, then I hate to break it to you . . .

He washed dirty feet. He lived to meet the needs of others. He made it clear that he didn't come to be served but to serve others (Mark 10:45).

THE DANGER OF INADEQUACY

There's an evil twin to a sense that we are entitled, and it's just as pervasive in many churches. The problem is not that you think of yourself more highly than you ought, but that you don't think of yourself very highly at all. Why is this a danger? Because those who feel inadequate tend to sit on the sidelines. They aren't sure God has a use for them, and they struggle to find a place in the church. You see, while entitlement is a very real danger, some churches develop their ministries to be so excellent and well produced, so polished, that there's no room left for the amateur servant. When only the best is acceptable, there's little room left for someone to explore their gifts and figure out where they might be used by God. In a church like this, people show up every week and watch the singers sing, the preacher preach, and the kids' workers working with the kids, and they think, *There is no way that I can do that.*

Like entitlement, our perceived disadvantages cause us to stop short of what God wants for us. We shrink back because of pride or fear. But again, that's where grace enters the picture. Grace counters our inadequacy because it affirms that while we aren't the most skilled or professional, we're still loved and accepted by God. Grace counters our pride because it reminds us that no matter how good we are at what we do, it's never good enough and it's all a gift that we never deserved. When we live in this grace, knowing that we're undeserving but accepted, we tend to be humble about our abilities yet not afraid to use them. We give grace to others. Because God has lavished his love on us by taking on the form of a servant and serving us, we can lavish love on others the same way. And one of the ways we do that is by serving the body.

But how?

Paul wrote in Romans 12:4, "As in one body we have many members, and the members do not all have the same function." Like a body, every part has a part to play. And while we don't all have the *same* role, we all have *some* role. Not all of us are going to be gifted in the same things. Not everyone has the gift of preaching. Not everyone is going to lead from the front. Not everyone is great with middle schoolers. Some roles are going to be more behind the scenes, but that doesn't make them any less important.

To help church members fully embrace their roles, we need to move beyond the myth of the super-Christian or superpastor. Maybe you've seen this mentality in the church before. It's where the paid staff—whether a single, gifted senior pastor or a team of folks in a larger church—are seen as the ones who get all the ministry done. The regular folks come on Sunday and drop some money in the offering plate each week to pay the bills, but it's the job of the staff of professional super-pastors to spring into action like little trained monkeys, teaching all the Bible studies, leading all the ministry efforts, and taking care of all the problems. After all, that's what they are being paid to do. Isn't it?

One problem with the super-Christian myth is that no one at your church has the time or the talent to tackle everything within the church. That's certainly true of me. There are certain things that I have a knack for, areas where God has gifted me, and things that fall into my skill set. But there are other areas where my role and contribution are just not going to be the same as those of others. Nobody wants me handling the budget, because ninth-grade math was the worst three years of my life. Nobody wants me leading worship, unless your church growth strategy is to actually make crowds disappear.

I'm encouraged when I see people who take up the mantle of ministry and don't view paid staff as hired help but as they are—facilitators, teachers, and equippers for the work of ministry. Paid staff are typically so focused on the needs of the church that they may struggle to reach beyond the walls of the building. Instead, it's the church members who are regularly interacting with people outside the church and are best suited to serve, lead, and minister in circles of influence far beyond what any staff member could ever do. Often the best outreach ideas a church has don't originate in a staff meeting; they begin where a church member saw a need, started serving, and then invited others in the church to join in.

Our jobs and roles pursuing the kingdom mission and purposes of God are not going to be the same. What God wires me to do, he may not necessarily wire you to do. And that's okay. The point is not that we have the *same* role, but we have *some* role. So don't forget: *you have a role*. Remember that.

We are working to build a culture where not only does everyone count, but everyone contributes. Turning back to Romans 12 again, verse 5 says, "So we, though many, are one body in Christ, and individually members one of another."

Paul's analogy of the body means that what one body part does affects all other body parts. You know this if you've ever stubbed your toe in the middle of the night. Every other part you have rushes to the aid of Mr. Toe. Mr. Brain sets off alarms to everybody else, letting them know Mr. Toe has temporarily gone off the reservation. Mr. Hand reaches down to comfort Mr. Toe, Mr. Foot begins to overcompensate by hopping up and down, and Mr. Mouth chimes in with—well, we won't say what Mr. Mouth chimes in with. But you get the point. What one member of the body does affect all the others.

. . . AND GRACE WILL LEAD ME HOME . . .

By this point, you understand the thread of grace in Scripture, you know that you've been given a spiritual gift, and you know that you need to put that gift into play. But at the crucial intersection of our theology and our practice, we need to still ask the question, "What do you do with what you know?"

Several Easters ago we faced the same problem many churches face: there were more people outside than we had room for inside. We had made all the right plans in the weeks leading up to Easter. We'd added more service times, made plans for additional venues, and encouraged our regulars to take advantage of some of those "off-peak" options. But when the day came, the most popular service time still proved to be the most popular service time, and five minutes into the service, we still had first-time guests standing on the sidewalk, wondering if there would be a spot for them in the auditorium.

I was the guy tasked with "scoot in" duty that day. It was my job to take the stage at a couple of strategic times toward the beginning of the service and remind people to fill in empty seats and leave space near the aisle.* The only problem was *there were no empty seats left*. As in none. Zip. Nada. We were at max capacity in our main venue, and we were about to send our honored guests down a long sidewalk to a secondary venue, one that was okay but certainly less enjoyable. Unfortunately, it wouldn't deliver the experience we'd designed for them.

I walked onstage, knowing that we didn't just need to fit a half dozen more people in. We needed to free up a hundred or so seats. I greeted everyone in the auditorium, delivered the typical Easter

---

* Yes, it's a ridiculously glamorous job. Be jealous.

salutations, and asked those who had been a part of our church for a year or more to stand up. A few hundred did so. Then I asked all of those who were seated to applaud all of those who had staying power at the church: these were the leaders, the movers and shakers, the go-getters. Wild applause and rampant adoration broke out. (Side note here: never miss an opportunity to play to people's egos. The year-or-mores were excited about the recognition.)

But then, just before the applause died down, I said this to the seasoned vets of our church: "If you're standing right now, then you probably consider yourself one of us. You've been here long enough that you are likely a covenant member or even a leader. And for that reason, I want you to lead by picking up your belongings, grabbing your spouse and family by the hands, and walking down to our additional venue so we can free up some seats for our honored guests."

Busted.

For some crazy reason, it worked (and I didn't get fired). The ego stroking helped identify those who should have listened to the instructions given in previous weeks, and now they had two choices: sit back down and be labeled as self-centered bums; or grab their stuff and go, marking them as servant-hearted people who valued a guest's comfort more than their own. I have no doubt that most of those who stood up that day knew what they *should* do. After all, we'd been harping on the need to free up space for our Easter guests for weeks. But they needed a flash-point moment to put knowledge into action. And that's the way personal discipleship works: we learn and learn and learn, and then eventually we have to act. As James 1:22 reminds us, we must be doers of the Word and not hearers only. We can't simply receive grace and never live out that grace. To quote the apostle Paul again, "You were called to freedom, brothers. Only do not use your freedom as an opportunity for the flesh, but *through love serve one another*. For the whole law is fulfilled in one word: 'You shall love your neighbor as yourself'" (Galatians 5:13–14, emphasis added).

If we've received love, we have to give love. Too many of us use the grace that we've been given as a get-out-of-jail-free card: it allows us to get forgiveness of any sin and gives us an out from being a servant. But that is a skewed and twisted view of grace. Paul told us that our freedom—the grace that is ours through Jesus—is not a get-out-of-jail-free card; neither is it a license to be the one who only gets served. No, those who get grace understand service. They understand that since we have been loved well, we must also love well.

We must put one more crucial piece of the grace puzzle into place. This piece helps us to see the full picture of grace when it's worked out in our lives. If we fail to recognize it, we run the risk of living stagnant lives, being people who always receive grace and never give it. In the second chapter of Philippians, Paul again pointed us back to—you guessed it—grace! He showed us how the promises that are ours in Christ don't simply stop with us but extend beyond us to others. He painted a picture that helps us see that Christ's example is our encouragement to be a living conduit of grace.

> Do nothing from selfish ambition or conceit, but in humility count others more significant than yourselves. Let each of you look not only to his own interests, but also to the interests of others. Have this mind among yourselves, which is yours in Christ Jesus, who, though he was in the form of God, did not count equality with God a thing to be grasped, but emptied himself, by taking the form of a servant, being born in the likeness of men. (Philippians 2:3–7)

Let me ask a probing question: Where does conceit arise in your own life? The KJV interprets *conceit* as "vainglory," a fun word that sounds like a villain from a James Bond movie.* Our vainglories always stem from our desire to have what we want when we want it. We want personal comfort, a sense of self-worth, a stake in the game, our name on a plaque, or a title with some power. Those vainglories can be blatantly obvious, like fighting and clawing to get ahead in our career. Or they can be subtle, like the loud sigh we deliver when the guy in front of us in the express lane has more than ten items.†

When we submit to the temptation of vainglory, we are *pursuing our glory*. This desire to be right or noticed or in charge stems from the idea that the grace of God is not enough for us—we still need to get more for ourselves using our own efforts. It's an idea that still hisses with the faint whispers of a snake in the garden of Eden. Seeking our own glory is a bottomless pit where we are constantly propping up ourselves and validating a million reasons that justify why we should be treated better or honored more.

As we saw in chapter 3, the only antidote for vainglory is humility. Paul tells us that humility asks us to consider others as more significant than ourselves. *More significant* doesn't imply that we have *no* significance; it simply prioritizes others first. Counting others as *more significant* means that we don't just take our own wants and needs into consideration when making a decision. Looking at a stranger as *more significant* means that we might set aside our schedule to help them. Seeing our spouse as *more significant* means that we sacrifice our greed for their good. Viewing people in our church as *more significant* means that we eschew personal preference for kingdom impact.

---

* Bond: "This is the end for you, Mr. Vainglory." Vainglory: "You can't kill me. I'm already dead."

† But seriously, Guy with Fifteen Items: knock it off. Nobody likes you.

If vainglory evolves from the belief that God's grace is not enough, where does humility come from? You guessed it. (You're so smart!) We can only live in humility when we know that God's grace is *more than enough.* His grace cements our identity and gives us purpose. His grace jettisons our need to prove ourselves and keeps our ambitions in check. His grace helps us to see others as more significant. Earlier in the New Testament, Paul reminded us that everything in life can be done not only for the glory of God, but for the good of others. He said that "whether you eat or drink . . . do all to the glory of God. Give no offense to Jews or to Greeks or to the church of God, just as I try to please everyone in everything I do, *not seeking my own advantage, but that of many, that they may be saved*" (1 Corinthians 10:31–33, emphasis added).

If you are a leader within the church, let me speak directly to you for a moment. You may be coming to the end of this chapter and your head is filling up with the faces of dozens of people in your congregation whom you believe to be corrupted by vainglory. Church has become all about them, and they have a tendency to criticize or stand in the way when a new initiative is pursued that will reach new people. May I remind you that you can't change those people? You can't. That is the role of the Holy Spirit. Your role is to pray that the Spirit would speak loudly and they would listen sensitively.

Please don't be afraid of the dissonance that is felt when a person becomes repelled by what initially attracted them. Use that dissonance as a teaching opportunity to explain the gospel once more. This is a chance for people to realize that what they enjoy about church results from someone else's service to them. Further, it's a chance to realize that when they submit themselves to the humble service of others, an even greater joy awaits them.

Friends, we need a new encounter with grace. That's the key

message of this book and the secret to an amazing guest ministry in your church. It can no longer be just about us, but about those who are coming after us. We can't simply be reservoirs; we must be conduits. The gospel is too precious and the mission is too great for us to continue with an inward focus and to maintain the status quo. If we buck up against this, the problem may not be our view of people on the outside; it might be a poor view of what God has done for us on the inside, in our hearts. So how do we solve this? The answer comes in understanding Jesus's mission, the reason he came to earth, and the part we play in the gospel story. As we conclude, we will see that Jesus came to seek and to save the lost.

Conclusion: Many Churches, One Mission

The plates still had food on them when Zacchaeus stood up from the table. In the initial whirlwind of activity after dropping down from the tree, he had somehow gotten a message to one of his servants and told him to stop whatever he was doing to prepare for company. The household staff jumped into action, expecting a traveling official from the Roman government or another tax-collecting crony to walk through the door. After all, that was the usual type of clientele Zacchaeus hosted. He had no friends. His family had distanced themselves from him. So for years, the only voices around the dinner table were quite literally partners in crime with the master of the house. The servants were tired of overhearing the scheming and the gloating, the new and devious ways to separate honest people from hard-earned wages, the tales of excess and greed and lascivious lifestyles.

And so it was with no small surprise that the servants looked up from their feverish preparation to see their boss walk through the door accompanied by an unfamiliar face. The man didn't have the appearance of a Roman or the finery that was usually associated with high-ranking officials. His countenance and kindness immediately separated him from the undesirables that normally consumed the food and showed contempt for the staff. One of the servants put two and two together and realized that the man at the table wasn't just any man, he was the man all of Judea was talking about. He was Jesus of Nazareth, and he was in the house where they worked, sitting at the table where they served, eating the food they had prepared.

Also surprising was the obvious change they could see overtaking their master. They were used to him being dismissive and demanding, and yet now he had an air of something that was almost like . . . *kindness?* It was unfamiliar, not something they were accustomed to experiencing at the hands of Zacchaeus. They had caught parts of the conversation: Zacchaeus asking questions about matters of life and matters of religion; Jesus referring to eternity and value and something he called "true riches." They had watched their boss listen intently with a range of emotions: seeming miserable and hopeful and sorrowful and joyful, looking down and looking away and leaning in. They had noticed neighbors and townspeople gathering around open windows and doorways, those who had followed along after the public display in town, curious and concerned that Jesus was associating with a man with such a vile reputation.

So when Zacchaeus took advantage of a brief lull in the conversation and stood, he had the attention of everyone: Jesus, servants, neighbors, townspeople. The corrupt tax collector raised his hand, and they all stopped to listen.

"Behold, Lord, the half of my goods I give to the poor. And if I have defrauded anyone of anything, I restore it fourfold" (Luke 19:8).

The reaction from the eavesdropping crowd was immediate and evident. "*If* I have defrauded!" "*If?*" Of *course* he had defrauded! The gathering was littered with those who had seen their wages disappear because of this man's greed. For him to say *if* he had defrauded would be like the Jordan River saying, "*if* I contained water." Rivers are wet and tax collectors are crooks. That is *what* and *who* they are.

But as their initial cynicism passed, the eavesdroppers realized that a change, an unbelievable transformation, had overtaken this particular *who*. Gone was Zacchaeus's pomp and pride. The bravado of his position was deflated. He no longer carried the posture of an all-powerful chief tax collector with the backing of the Roman government. Rather, he looked like a vulnerable child in the presence of his protective big brother. Zacchaeus's declaration pointed back to his obvious transgressions and greed. He was admitting his offenses against those gathered as well as the countless names and faces he had forgotten. But he also pointed forward to the action he would take as a part of his new perspective, his new commitment to living differently. Half of his goods—not just his salary but half of his worldly possessions—would be liquidated to take care of the poor. And he would make amends to those he had stolen from, reimbursing not only what he had taken, but *four times* that amount.

As some of the servants did the math in their heads, they realized that Zacchaeus would make himself a pauper if he followed through on his promise. In a moment he would go from being the wealthiest man in Jericho to penniless, the one who gave everything away. But then the servants and the neighbors saw Jesus rise from the table, throw his arm around Zacchaeus's shoulder, and declare words that his host never dreamed he would hear: "Today salvation has come to this house, since he also is a son of Abraham" (Luke 19:9).

• • •

We would be hard-pressed to find a more appropriate use of the word *salvation* anywhere in the four gospels. What happened in Zacchaeus's home and heart that day was nothing short of a miracle. Here was a tax collector who had everything yet was responsible for the poverty and scorn of his neighbors and kinsmen. To those around him, he was the least likely to admit his need for help, and the least likely to receive help from a man as righteous as Jesus.

And so *salvation* is an entirely appropriate descriptor. Jesus did for Zacchaeus what Zacchaeus could never do for himself. He thrust his arm deep into the depravity of Zacchaeus's soul and saved him from his own hopelessness. He took a lifetime of greed and shame and replaced it with generosity and grace. He removed a stony, cold, hard heart and gave him an entirely new wellspring of life. For all of Zacchaeus's riches and scheming and power, what he really needed was a savior. The most hated had become the dearly loved. The one whom everyone had written off suddenly had the grace of God written on his heart.

As we have journeyed together through the pages of this book, my prayer has been that your eyes have been open to see the various representations of Zacchaeus in your own community. You'll see him in the eyes of the one everyone else has dismissed. You'll notice her hanging her head in shame because of the sins of her past. You'll recognize them perched precariously in a tree, straining to get a glimpse of hope when their self-sufficiency is no longer enough.

And I trust that you have been forced to reckon with your own identity as I have had to reckon with mine: I am often a religious insider who looks down on—or at least doesn't look out for—those who are on the outside. I've labeled certain people as beyond the reach of the long arm of God's grace. I've determined that there are specific undesirables that Jesus would never know by name, much less want to share a meal with.

The final pronouncement we see in the Luke 19 account is the most important one of the story. In verse 10 Jesus sums up his entire three-year ministry, the reason he spent three decades on earth, and ultimately God's plan for his Son from the beginning of time:

"The Son of Man came to seek and to save the lost."

To the doubters in the crowd that day, that one sentence from Jesus was likely confusing. Some of them viewed Jesus as a wise teacher, others as a troublemaker, still others as the one who would remove the shackles of a foreign government. But Jesus dismissed all of those things and said that his mission, his one thing, his driving motivation and mandate, was to seek lost people and to save lost people. He found people who realized they were utterly helpless and needed a helper. He sought out people who were dead and made them alive. He took darkness and made it light.

"The Son of Man came to seek and to save the lost."

When salvation came, transformation followed. Tax collectors became benefactors, Pharisees became followers, and Zealots became zealous for what really mattered in eternity. Adulterous women were told to go and sin no more. Fishermen started baiting and casting for a different type of fish. A band of temperamental, fearful, doubtful misfits became the builders of a global church that is still in existence two millennia later.

"The Son of Man came to seek and to save the lost."

As we've looked at the story of Zacchaeus, I hope you've seen and experienced a taste of Jesus's mission. Jesus didn't come for good people; he came for broken people. He didn't preoccupy himself with those on the inside; he went to the margins, to those on the fringe, to those on the outside. Jesus's mission is now our mission. You won't die on a cross for the sins of the world, but Jesus calls you to deny yourself, take up your cross, and follow him. He calls you to embrace his work of serving people in love, of sharing the good news about God's offer of forgiveness, pointing people to Jesus. Jesus calls you to be a witness among your friends and family, but also in your neighborhood, in the workplace, and among the nations. If he loved people, if he came to seek the lost, then as his followers we must do the same.

And while we can join Jesus in *seeking* the lost, the job of *saving* the lost is totally up to Jesus. We don't save, but one way we seek is by clearing the path to involvement in the local church so that the one who does save is easily seen. We can identify those in the crowd who need to see Jesus. We can identify where our churches and our gatherings have built-in barriers that inadvertently keep people from recognizing who Jesus is. Through years of tradition and self-protection, we may have created unnecessary offenses that keep outsiders out. If we are going to proactively seek the lost, we have to identify and remove those barriers.

At the same time, we must realize that the one offense that we cannot and should not remove is the message of the gospel. It is the caged lion that is completely sufficient to defend itself. It is the one thing our guests may not initially like but desperately need. We seek the lost by understanding that details of the church weekend and how we run our churches and organizations really do matter. What we say or don't say and do or don't do will either add to or take away from the songs we sing and the sermons we preach. For our guests, the sermon really does start in the parking lot, and our lack of preparation and forethought can turn them off to the gospel before they have a chance to explicitly hear the gospel.

Our care for those on the outside must include the admission that we don't always like those who aren't like us. Whether our issue is with sin or lifestyle choices or political persuasions, we are all too quick to label others and distance ourselves. Rather than rushing to the wounded, we are content to run away from the battle, hide behind our so-called tribe, and lob missives from the fortresses of social media and fearmongering. We have to grasp the power of hospitality and kindness as a lost apologetic, genuinely loving those whom Jesus loves.

As we seek the lost, we must come to terms with the reality that the way we serve others can't be an end unto itself. It can't be a cul-de-sac, the destination of our journey. Individual and institutional hospitality has to be a catalyst, a neon signpost that points others to the gospel. The kindness of our congregations should always be a reflection of the kindness that Jesus has shown to us. We know that we have first been loved by him, which frees us to love others.

We have to take a hard look in the mirror and see the older brother staring back at us. Sometimes it is going to feel as though seeking the good of the lost is at odds with seeking our own good. But the party the Father throws is one that is open to all and can be enjoyed by all. Our perspective has to change as we realize that the grace that is given to the lost is the same grace that was given to and now sustains us.

And finally, seeking the lost forces us to remember that there is always room at the table. The Holy Spirit can use our gifts and our lives to have an impact on the lives of others. We don't have to shrink back because of inadequacy or step back because of entitlement. The grace of God can flow through us to serve other people and draw others to him.

We don't know the last chapter of Zacchaeus's life. We don't know if the proclamations he made at his dinner table were carried out in the weeks and years to come. We don't know his setbacks or his successes. We don't have the perspective to see how his story ended. We don't know the extent of his redemption or the change in his reputation. We just know that Jesus said that Zacchaeus was a part of his mission, that Zacchaeus was one of the lost he came to seek and to save. I don't know about you, but I've never known one of Jesus's promises to go unfulfilled.

So while you may not know the last chapter of Zacchaeus's life, you do know the chapter that God is writing with your life right now. As you have read, you have undoubtedly identified areas in your church—and in your life—that need some attention. You have made a mental list of things that have to change. Maybe you have taken inspiration from "Pastor Walter" and decided to start paying attention to the details your guests are already seeing. You may have discovered some tendencies in your own life where you're not showing the kindness of Jesus to those you consider to be on the outside. You have likely seen some older brother tendencies surface, and you're trying to figure out what repentance looks like in those situations.

Friends, I don't know you. I probably don't know your church. And I can only guess at your context. But I know the commission we've been given: if you are a follower of Christ or a member of his church, you and I are called to seek the lost. Those of us on the inside must be champions for those still on the outside. The way we treat our guests matters. It's not just about building our churches or increasing attendance. What we do on the weekend has echoes in eternity. Souls are at stake that are far more valuable than our cherished traditions, our personal preferences, our comfort zones, or our older-brotherness.

The way I set up the weekend gathering won't look like the way you would do it. It's not going to be the same in every church everywhere. You and your fellow church members will have to wrestle and pray and try and fail and try again when it comes to serving guests in your context. Whether you're a storefront church plant with a dozen people in metal folding chairs or the tenth campus of a megachurch with an enormous budget and infrastructure, whether you're in rural Mississippi or in downtown LA or in a tiny apartment in Beijing, whether you're just getting started or tweaking an existing system, what you do will look different from what someone else is doing who is reading this book somewhere else. For as many different churches that are represented by the readers of this book, there are as many different ways to implement what you've hopefully learned through it.

So rather than adapt to a formula, cut and paste a few principles, or tackle a list of action steps, take just one action step: imitate Jesus. Let's remember that the one who sought us is still seeking others. Let's keep in mind that the Great Commission doesn't just challenge us to make disciples at the ends of the earth but in our backyards. Let's be salt and light, love people well, and set our weekend services up for great hospitality. Let's pray that the Holy Spirit will see fit to use us and our flaws and our missteps, and take our willingness and our openness and work through us to reach others. And let's look forward to the day when we can joyfully look in the face of those who were formerly on the outside and gladly proclaim, "Salvation has come to this house."

People were the mission of Jesus, and people are still our mission today. Let's love them because we understand just how much he has loved us.

Appendix: Getting Started and Starting Over

So what now?

You've reached the end of the book (unless you're the kind of person who skips straight to the appendix*), and if your book-reading habits are anything like mine, you're not exactly sure what happens next. When I get to the last page of a book, I'm either supremely thankful that I survived or eager to apply what I've learned. Maybe you're that way too. Hopefully what you're feeling right now is anticipation about the application.

We've talked about philosophies behind guest services, theoretical reasons for why hospitality within the local church is important, and biblical mandates for welcoming the stranger. Perhaps you've underlined a few sentences or highlighted a few takeaways or even used your reading app to clip a few passages into Evernote. My prayer is that you've learned a lot and laughed a little, and you've been inspired to take the next step to improve the guest awareness culture at your church.

But now that you're at the end, what will you do with what you know?

---

* Sicko.

We've spent a lot of time on the *why*, but I want to make sure you're well equipped to tackle the *how*: How do you improve an existing guest services culture, or how do you build one from the ground up? That's the $100,000 question, and I don't want to be guilty of giving you a one-size-fits-all answer. The way you approach guest services at Possum Holler Baptist in Lick Skillet, Tennessee, is going to look different than the way you'd approach it at Megakingdom World Outreach Center in Chicago, Illinois.

Before I talk about *getting started*, it might be helpful if we talk about what it looks like to *start over*. Because in some ways, that's the harder path. If you've ever attempted to remodel a house, you know just what I mean. Sometimes it's easier to buy some gasoline and a pack of matches and just light, flick, and walk away.*

Starting over may need to happen if you're in a church with an existing guest services culture but it's a toxic one. By *toxic*, I mean that the institutional structures for hospitality are no longer helpful to those on the outside but rather exist to serve those who are comfortably assimilated inside. Toxic cultures come to the surface when church members don't embrace guests who are unlike them. They show themselves when sermons focus on the sins and evils of the world and fail to acknowledge the remaining sin and unbelief in the pews. They can even be evident when congregations refuse to give up outdated modes of ministry because of the familiar comfort they get via the "good old days." And a toxic culture can even be seen in a place we don't expect: when a church tries *too hard* to make guests feel welcome, smothering them and pressuring them to get involved before they're ready.

I might have just described your congregation, and by doing so I certainly don't mean to discourage you. I have found that most

---

* On second thought, that's arson. Don't do that.

churches aren't as much unkind as they are unaware. When pressed on the issue, very few authentic followers of Jesus would say that they don't like those on the outside. Applying the label of "toxic" to their church would be heartbreaking because they don't want to stand in the way of someone feeling welcomed by the church and eventually coming to salvation. These toxic churches don't mean to be toxic; it's just that over the years, poor habits and passive behaviors have crept in and threaten to keep outsiders out.

If you are a leader in a toxic church and want to get rid of the toxicity, I encourage you to do so with tremendous gentleness and humility. Do it by changing behavior rather than castigating people. Go back to the "older brother" story in chapter 5. Remember that because we have been great receivers of grace, we must also be great dispensers of grace. Start conversations with church members that are meant to cast vision rather than aspersion. Lay out plans that are inclusive rather than exclusive. You have the opportunity to see the Holy Spirit open the eyes of congregation members and give them a new heart for guests from our community. So don't short-circuit his work by trying to whip people into shape rather than lovingly leading them as a shepherd.

But let's be realistic: when we start over, some learned behaviors will have to be unlearned. That's sometimes easier said than done. Church members will have to start looking at the inside from the perspective of an outsider. They will have to ask, "If I were to come here for the first time—not having any of the relationships that I have now or knowing what I know—would I feel welcomed? Would I want to come back?" They will have to take long looks at what is not working and prayerfully begin to right the ship. But more than anything, church members who are committed to unlearn behavior will have to die to their personal comfort constantly in exchange for the comfort of a guest.

Now that we've talked a bit about starting over, I think we can begin to get on the same page and address what it means to get started. The following list is not exhaustive or absolute. You won't be able to tackle all of these at once. You might complete the first one or two items quickly and then slowly implement the rest over the course of months or years. Some things you may opt never to do, and some things may be replaced with a much better idea you or your team discovers. The point is, you should feel free to cut and paste the principles, but you'll have to look at your own context and specific needs to form the particulars. If I were starting a guest services team in a church for the very first time, these are the big rocks I would want to put in place.

Decide Who Owns It

Hospitality in your church won't just happen. If your congregation's guest awareness is going to increase, someone will have to be the champion for it, the cheerleader behind it, and the coach of it. If you've made it all the way through this book, that someone might just be you.[*]

A church planter once told me that when they had fewer than fifty people in their first months, guest services was no problem. In fact, the concern was that guests might feel a little overwhelmed at the attention they received. Because it was easy to spot who was new—and because of the excitement that comes along with a church plant—every first-time guest was spoken to, cared for, and made to feel like a part of the family from their first visit.

But he said that something strange happened about the time they hit fifty people. Suddenly everyone's job became no one's job. A first-time guest would walk in the door, and dozens of pairs of eyes

---

[*] Good job, you!

would look at them and then look around at each other, wondering who would be the first to greet the new kid. It was awkward for the congregation because no one knew who should step up. And it was awkward for the guest because they weren't sure why no one was talking to them.

So decide who is in charge, who will be held accountable, who will be given the responsibility for the hospitality culture in your church. This person needs to have the right mix of people skills and administrative skills. They don't necessarily need to be a raging extrovert or a spreadsheet Jedi,* but they do need to be able to model hospitality for their team and keep up with their team rosters, training schedules, and guest follow-up.

Find Your Stakeholders

Even though someone needs to be in charge, that doesn't mean someone can do it alone. Look around your congregation for people who naturally exude hospitality. Find those who leverage influence among the people in the pews. Ask them to consider joining you in forming the nucleus of a team to improve the culture of your church. And then begin to learn together. Pass around your copy of this book (or buy 'em their own—I won't complain). Visit other churches together to see what they're doing, and borrow ideas liberally.

As you meet together and learn together, dream together. Talk through what your core values for hospitality will be. Rally around some key, easy-to-remember phrases or Scripture verses. Think about the number of volunteers you might need on a weekend and the various tasks people will undertake.

Use your stakeholders to see things you might not see and talk to people you might not know. As you cast your initial vision, you

---

* "I find your lack of formulas disturbing."—Darth Variable

will have blind spots, so humbly ask them to poke holes in your plan. It's better to have a few trusted friends spot the problems early on than have the vision derailed once it has launched.

Begin with the End in Mind

Ask this question: "If time, money, resources, and volunteers had no limit, what would we want our guest services team to look like?" I get it—that's a laughable question for all of us, no matter the size of our churches or our budgets. It seems there is *never* enough money or people to do all that we can dream up. Nevertheless, I want you to start from a surplus mentality rather than a scarcity mentality. Too often we try to just scrape by with the minimum effort for ministry. And while it may be true that all you have right now is the minimum, I'd caution you against getting *used to* the minimum.

Instead, utilize your stakeholders for a brainstorming session. Set a few goals for the types of teams you'd like to have, the number of volunteers that would make a robust team, or what you want your guest reception area to look like. Write them down. Create an ideal timeline, and then start working toward your goals. You won't get there overnight. But every once in a while when you glance up at those lists thumbtacked to your corkboard or come across that plan in your file drawer, you'll be reminded of what the dream originally looked like. When that happens, I hope it will shake you out of the ruts you'll inevitably find yourself in. I also hope you'll find that your dreams for your ministry will be bigger than they started, based on what you've learned about serving the guests in your church.

Train the *Why* before the *What*

Quality training for volunteers is essential. We should equip them in the classroom and let them observe us on the front lines before we turn them loose and wish them well. Few things are more frustrating to a volunteer than to be given a task with no context or background for it. When a volunteer doesn't know the basics of their job and doesn't have anyone to ask, they will very quickly lose interest in the job and walk away.

It's easy to give a volunteer a job description and tell them to get to work. Anyone can assign a task. And truthfully, just about anyone can execute a task. But one of the marks of a good leader is not just assigning mundane tasks but creating a compelling vision. That vision—that *why*—will sometimes tether a volunteer to a job even when the task gets a little tough.

In our context, our *why* is the gospel. We tell every potential volunteer that their primary job is not to hold open doors or to help people find a seat; it is to demonstrate the grace of the gospel. We show them how the sermon starts in the parking lot and how the messages a guest hears or sees on the sidewalk will either add to or take away from the messages they hear from the stage. I always find it fascinating when volunteers come into one of our trainings expecting to learn the finer points of serving on the parking team. I mean, it's relatively easy: look for the open spots and point the cars in that direction. Boom! You're trained. What's much harder is to help a forty-seven-year-old volunteer remember that regardless of rain or heat or distracted drivers, their primary job is not to remember how to park cars but to remember the heart behind *why* they're parking cars.

Now we turn our attention to the nuts and bolts of the guest experience. Even with trained volunteers, guests may not give your church a chance if they don't feel like you've prepared for them. I mentioned some of these things at the end of chapter 2 but covered them in the form of multiple rapid-fire questions. Here in the appendix, I thought I'd dispense with the question marks and make a few suggestions instead.

Check Your Online Presence

In our digital age, many people check out a place online before they check it out in person. I can browse a new food truck's menu or read reviews on a potential plumber* from the comfort of my iDevice. The same goes for our churches. For the sake of your guests, your landing page should be simple and to the point. If possible, include a clip from a service so guests will know exactly what to expect, and make it easy for a potential guest to submit a question. Your service times and location should be up to date, and for the love of Rand McNally, *please* include your city and state. I'm surprised at how many First Methodist websites list their location on Main Street. No city. No state. Just Main Street.†

If you maintain other social media accounts—Twitter, Facebook, Instagram, etc.—the only advice I'd offer is to *maintain them*. Keep them up to date. Engage with people. Don't let inquiries go unanswered. If you don't want to use them, chuck them. The only thing worse than no social media presence is a social media presence that hasn't been updated in eleven months.

Examine Your Approach

If you had never been to your church, would you know where to go? People who drive by your facility every day on their way to work or school may not actually know it's there. Just because you've had a multidecade run in your community, don't assume that people can find you. Use signage (permanent during the week and extra temporary signage on the weekend) to let people know where you are.

When someone drives onto your property, they should see a clean facility and well-kept grounds. You don't have to compete

---

* "He's #1 in the #2 business."

† That's right, webmaster: I'm sure you're the only First Methodist out there.

with the manicured botanical garden on the other side of town, but you at least need to pull a few weeds, slap on a fresh coat of paint, and move the eyesore church van out of the front parking lot.

Pay Attention to Parking

You may not be ready for a parking team. But if you're thinking about one, here are a few things to consider. Parking volunteers may not need to be functional as much as they are friendly, waving to passersby and giving first-time guests the confidence they've arrived at the right place.

Consider a way for first-timers to identify themselves so you can give them a parking spot close to the entrance. We use signs that encourage them to turn on their hazard lights. Only about 50 percent of our guests actually do that,* but for those who do it's a seamless way to make sure they don't wander to a parking area far from where we want them to be.

Church leaders should park far away from the building and leave the best spaces for guests. Unfortunately, the Bible is silent on the subject of front-and-center reserved parking spaces for pastors, but I'm pretty sure I can make a convincing case for why Peter would have dismounted his donkey well before he got to the upper room.

Take a Look at Your Outer Entry

Will your guests know which entrance is for them? Strategically placed signage is helpful (and I highly recommend it), but signs never replace people. Greeters should populate your sidewalk and main entrance doors to help guests navigate directions. And speaking of doors: I believe that you can drastically improve your

---

* The other 50 percent probably can't find the button that makes their lights flash.

guest services culture by just eighteen inches. That's roughly the distance between a volunteer who stands *inside* the door and one who stands *outside*. It's a much nicer touch for a guest to see you before they get inside. Pull the door open as they approach rather than pushing it open just as they reach out to take the handle. It's a small but significant improvement.

Develop a First-Time-Guest Kiosk

Create a space specifically for your guests, a place designed to serve them in their earliest moments on site. If weather permits in your area, I recommend an outdoor tent located obnoxiously close to the main entrance. The tent should be clearly marked with "First time?" "New here?" or something similar. Why an outside tent? Guests are far more comfortable stopping at a somewhat neutral spot before they walk into an unfamiliar building. Staff the tent with your kindest and most helpful volunteers, and commission them to engage in conversations, answer questions about the church, and escort guests to their final destination.

Offer a Gift

At the tent, it's a really nice touch to offer a gift. I get it . . . every church in America has their own branded coffee mug.* But it's still nice to receive something. Include *just enough* literature in the gift bag so your guests know what *you* want them to know and what *they* want to know. Information on kids' and student ministries and small groups and newcomers events or classes is most often appreciated. *Do not* give them a forty-seven-page directory of every single small group, a church membership application, or an

---

* For a fun Saturday scavenger hunt, visit the thrift stores in your area and see how many of your church coffee mugs you find on the shelves. It's rather humbling. (Or at least that's what my friend from . . . um . . . some other church . . . told me.) But please, don't rebuy and reuse. Let it go, man.

outdated flyer from last spring's women's conference. Overloading them with too much information—or good information at the wrong time—is overwhelming.

May I let you in on a little secret?* We don't give our guests a gift bag because we're supergenerous. We give it to them because it's an easy way to know for certain they're a guest. That gift bag marked with our church logo is *only* used for first-time guests. When I see someone carrying one around, I can walk up to them assured that, no, we've never met before, and yes, I can introduce myself and offer to help them find their way around. The guest feels cared for, and I feel good about the fact I didn't reintroduce myself to someone for the sixth time.

Find a Way to Connect

We ask for minimal information (name, date of birth, email, phone number) at our first-time-guest tent. It works for us. In your context, it might be too invasive. You might experiment with cards in the pew racks, online registration, opportunities to text their information to a digital platform, or something else. Whatever method you use, don't be shy about getting to know your guests and letting them get to know you. We'll come back to this in the "Follow Up" section below.

Bring in Your Family Ministry

The guest experience shouldn't be limited to the guest services team. Partner with your kids' and student ministries to develop aligned systems of care. For example: if you ask for information at the first-time-guest kiosk, don't ask parents to fill out that exact same information five minutes later in the kids' lobby. Train your

---

* No, not the fact that I just procrastin-ate a half tub of Häagen-Dazs Toasted Coconut Caramel ice cream while writing this appendix. *Another* secret.

guest services teams so they know the classroom locations and can easily help guests find their way there.

Remind kids' volunteers of the importance of speaking to *both* the child and the parent. Consider having a standard script for parents that covers security procedures, asks about allergies, and describes what kids will be doing during the service. For middle school and high school volunteers, offer to answer any questions parents might have, and let them know about upcoming events where their student might be able to build deeper relationships with other kids in the group.

Think through Your Auditorium Entry

Don't relegate the role of auditorium door greeter to simply handing out bulletins and ink pens. Use this team to set the tone for what is to come. If the service hasn't started yet, a warm greeting is appropriate. If the service is under way or if the congregation is in the middle of a reflective moment, the entry volunteer can help interpret what's happening and either hold the guest in the lobby (if the auditorium is dark) or hand them off to a member of the seating team (if the auditorium is full). This team should also maintain doors, shutting them when the lobby gets too loud or the auditorium's lights are down.

Set Up a Seating Team

Like your parking team, the seaters may not need to be as functional as they are just friendly. If you normally have a crowd of two hundred in an auditorium that seats six hundred, a choreographed team will just get annoying.* But if you normally deal with huge

---

* I once saw a volunteer stop two people to ask how many were in their party. At the time, there were literally hundreds of open seats in the auditorium. Settle down, there, Pharaoh. Let those people go.

crowds, a good seating team is worth their weight in gold. They can intercept early arrivers and encourage them to move to the front of the auditorium and the center of each row, leaving space in the rear and aisles for those who will come later. They can help moms with infants who may need to slip out, elderly individuals who can't walk long distances, or children with sensory issues to find the seat that is just right for them. Once the service is under way, they can further assist those who need to leave or handle disturbances that might arise.

Have a Next Steps Area

Whether first-time guests or longtime members, everyone needs a spot to go to when they have a question, need to sign up for an event, or figure out what's next in their journey. Equip your information table volunteers with information. Nothing is more frustrating to a guest than to ask a question of someone who doesn't have any answers. Scratch that: one thing is more frustrating, and that's being a volunteer who gets all the questions without knowing any answers. Train them well. Develop a cheat sheet. Let them know anything that might be announced from the stage that they may get questions about. Mention the information table frequently from the stage as a place to go to continue the conversation. And speaking of mentions from the stage . . .

Don't Forget Your Stage and Sermon

Every pastor, worship leader, and announcement person should be reminded that guests are in the room. Every single weekend, leadership should plan moments in the service to talk directly to guests. I'm not advocating for someone to call out a guest from the stage or embarrass them. I am saying that a few things are always helpful. Plan for a general welcome ("If you are with us for the first time, we are so thankful you're here"), next steps ("Maybe you saw the tent on the way in and weren't sure what it was for. I'd encourage you to stop by as you leave for a free gift"), and specific instructions ("At this time in our service, we are going to take up an offering. This is a time for the people of God to give generously to the mission of God. If you are our guest, we don't want you to feel compelled to give in any way; we're just glad you're here").

And by the way, should you talk to guests if you don't *have* guests? In most cases, yes. You're sending a subtle reminder to your congregation that this is a place for those on the outside. And if you talk to guests like they're there, eventually they will be.

Follow Up

You have a guest's information. Now what do you do with it? It all depends on your context. I grew up in a town where everybody from preacher to pagan knew that Monday night was church visitation night. If you showed up at a new church on Sunday, somebody from that church was going to be on your living room couch on Monday, guaranteed.

That may or may not work in your ministry setting. It doesn't work in ours. We rely on a simple series of one phone call and two follow-up emails with specific next steps. Our college staff will often contact college guests via text messaging. The point is not *how* you do it, it's *that* you do it. Thank them for coming, invite them back, and offer to answer any questions they have.

Turn Friends into Family

Finally, think about what's next for your guest. We've talked a lot about next steps. What are yours? Do you have a newcomers' event, a guest reception, or an offer of dinner with the pastor? Not every first-time guest will become a fully involved member of your church. But you should build enough on-ramps so that it's easy for them to do so. Be a personal advocate for the guests in your congregation, and help them take short, easy, achievable steps toward involvement. Don't pester them, but pastor them as they decide if your church is right for them. Offer a hand wherever and whenever you can, and give them grace as they begin the journey.

A few pages ago, I cautioned you that this "how to" wouldn't be one-size-fits-all. And here at the end I'd like to bring it up again. You likely have ideas that are vastly improved over what I've laid out. You may be in a specific scenario where some, if not most, of these suggestions simply won't work. I don't want to give you a formula, but I do want you to get started. Gather your stakeholders, refine your vision, make your plans, train your volunteers. And as you do, pray for wisdom and clarity on the best way to reach the guests in your city. However you approach it, wherever you land on your methodology, *just do something*. Love the people in your city. Roll out the red carpet to make them feel welcome on your turf. Establish on-ramps for them to move from connected to committed. And do it all not to make much of your church, not to grow your attendance, but to love people well and to make much of Jesus.

Acknowledgments

Some people will tell you that writing a book is hard. (I don't necessarily know who "some people" are, but they're out there. Trust me.) And I suppose they're partially right. Writing a book is ridiculously hard. Or at least it was for me. Step one involves an internal conversation in which you convince yourself, "This is a great idea; you should totally make this into a book!" Steps two through seventeen involve a lot of procrastinating and doing things more important than publishing what you believe to be a life-changing message, such as alphabetizing your soup cans. In step eighteen, you write the manuscript / find a publisher / cry over the publisher's edits / choose a book cover / wonder when (not if) you'll find the book in a dollar bin at a local bookstore. And in step nineteen, you rally your feelings when you realize that if you see your book in a dollar bin, that has to mean it is actually *in* a bookstore. So there's that.

But as hard as steps one through eighteen are, nothing compares to the abject fear that comes with thanking those who helped make the book. Because let's face it: this may be the only book I ever write; this is my only chance to thank people in print, and I am definitely going to forget someone. I've made lists as I've gone along and revisited every square inch of my memory bank, but I can guarantee you someone was left out. If that someone is you, please know that truly you are my second favorite person on the planet.

It's just that all of these other people tied for first.

Let's talk about that publishing team at Zondervan: Ryan Pazdur, Matt Johnson, Nathan Kroeze, Trinity McFadden, Sue Johnson, Lori Vanden Bosch, and Robert Hudson: thanks for taking a chance on an unknown and unpublished author with a crazy idea that just might work. (Maybe. We'll see.) You shaped so much of this content and made it look better than it ever would have otherwise, and you made the process mostly pain-free. I'm sorry about the things I said about you deep in my heart. I didn't mean them, really. It was the deadlines talking.

I stand on the shoulders of some incredible giants in the church guest services world. Mark Waltz: you're the godfather of this new generation. I'm grateful that you've poured out your life and let all of us learn from you. Bob Adams, Jason Young, and the rest of my G.E.N.E. compatriots, there's no one smarter than you. And to the hundreds of leaders who have hung with me in Weekenders, Workshops, Confabs, and consultations, this book exists because you let me bounce the ideas off of you first. Thank you.

The guest services volunteers at the Summit Church are my heroes. Every week hundreds of you show up to welcome those on the outside and pave the way toward the gospel. There's also a smaller group—our High-Capacity Volunteers (HCVs) who have journeyed with me through much of this content on way-too-early Cohort mornings over the past several years. The coffee was always terrible, but the conversation was always inspiring. I love every single one of you. Thanks for letting me tell the story of what God is doing through you.

Over the years there has been a mix of both paid and unpaid staff who have led in creating great experiences at our campuses. Many are still here, but some have gone on to spread the love at other churches or organizations all over the map. With all of them,

I've had the chance to interact with world-class leaders who love Jesus and love his people. I am grateful for your frontline (and often thankless) work every weekend.

My amazing "central staff" team currently consists of Marilyn Marrero and A. J. Farthing. But throughout the course of writing, I've cycled through other greats like Lori Perdue, Monica Hughston, and Kristy and Bradley Norris (apparently I'm a terrible human being to work for, and no one lasts). All of you made it possible for me to sneak in a little writing here and there. Thank you for picking up the slack I left behind.

Throughout this process I was surrounded by a phenomenal and long-suffering reading team who offered suggestions and edits to make the book better. David Talbert and Clayton Greene may as well have been listed as coauthors because their contribution to ideas and content was invaluable. To Jenn Curry, Jason Gaston, Abbi Hanks, Jonathan Lenker, Mike McKee, Matt Pearson, and Aaron Turner: thanks for all of the feedback, even when you said hurtful things like, "This isn't fit to shred and put in a hamster cage." I know you were kidding. Or maybe you weren't. Either way, I forgive you.

I had an unofficial advisory board of friends and writing pros who gave me just the right counsel and encouragement at just the right time. Andy and Heather Beckman, Ryan Doherty, Jonathan Edwards, Ashley Gorman, Brad Hambrick, Rob Laughter, Dana Leach, Jason Mathis, Mike McDaniel, Darin and Tori Meece (and the rest of the Meece small group), Josh Miller, Cas Monaco, Chris Pappalardo, Tiffany Pollard, Chuck Reed, Spence Shelton, Bonnie Shrum, Todd Unzicker, Jonathan Welch, and Curt and Hilary Yeo: thank you for answering every last one of my dumb questions and talking me down off the ledge when necessary.

The men and women of the Summit staff are more than coworkers; they are family. I'm so grateful to be able to serve alongside you.

There are way too many of us to call out, but I'm going to chance a few: Rick Langston: thanks for being the first one to suggest giving me a job and then teaching me how to be a better pastor. David Thompson: thanks for being such a great cheerleader throughout this project (that skirt is adorable on you). Chris Gaynor: I still don't think we look alike, but if I have half the love for Jesus as you do when I grow up, that's enough for me. Will Toburen and Jason Douglas: you swapped custody of me halfway through this project, but both of you were tremendously supportive through it all, and I'm grateful. To the Weekend Ministries Team—Jason Douglas, Curtis Andrusko, Jillian Boland, Justin Manny, and Gardner Pippin—there is no finer team of professionals / sideshow freaks that I've ever had the pleasure of working alongside. Thanks for humoring this old man and getting me out of meetings early enough so I can get to the cafeteria. And to my pastor, J. D. Greear: you're a leader who leaders love to lead under. Thank you for giving us the space to run and for constantly showing us Jesus.

I was doubly blessed to be raised in a family that modeled hospitality and then to marry into a family that did the same. David, Lindsey, Lauren, Lexy, Mikey, Alaina, Rob, Debbie, Kerry, Dane, Candace, Ronin, Rayne Mallory, Anna, Harper, Jackson, Lance, Kearsie, Emma, and Addie: you're a fun bunch to gather 'round the table with. Reitzel and Ginger: thank you for letting me marry your daughter and for showing me what it means to always have an open chair (even if Ozzie is in it most of the time). Sandra: you inherited a whole mess of us; thanks for loving us well (and for all the cinnamon bread). Mom: from my earliest days, you modeled what it meant to love others. I miss you and can't wait to see you again someday. And Dad: you always taught us to "kill 'em with kindness." I've watched you do that for over four decades, and I couldn't have had a better teacher.

Serving guests well isn't just something I write about; it's something I see my family demonstrate every single day. Haven: you never, ever meet a stranger, and you inspire me to be more adventurous in making friends. Jase: your behind-the-scenes work every weekend ensures that our first-time guests feel well loved. Austin: I love that you love to create great visuals that tell incredible stories and draw people in. Jacob: you and that dorky orange vest are a force to be reckoned with. Thanks for using your skills and your expertise in the parking lot. And Merriem: it's impossible to calculate how many thousands of first-timers you've helped assimilate into the life of our church over the years. If there's a "first face" people see on the weekend, I'm glad it's such a cute one. I love you.

And most importantly, to Jesus: you sought me when I was a stranger. You changed an enemy to a friend and a slave to a son. You made me your mission, and I'm eternally in awe.

Notes

Introduction

1. Rick Warren, *The Purpose Driven Church: Growth without Compromising Your Message and Mission* (Grand Rapids: Zondervan, 1995), 131–32.
2. Nelson Searcy, *Fusion: Turning First-Time Guests into Fully-Engaged Members of Your Church* (Ventura, CA: Regal, 2007), 105.
3. Gary L. McIntosh, *Beyond the First Visit: The Complete Guide to Connecting Guests to Your Church* (Grand Rapids: Baker, 2006), 14.
4. The term *seeker* appears in scores of church growth books from the 1990s, but one of the earliest I could find was from Robert E. Logan, *Beyond Church Growth: Action Plans for Developing a Dynamic Church* (New York: Revell, 1989), 65.
5. Jon Acuff, *Stuff Christians Like* (Grand Rapids: Zondervan, 2010), 103. (And yes, he took a genius swipe at our church—The Summit—in that summary. Well played, Jon. Well played indeed.)
6. Patrick Keifert, *Welcoming the Stranger: A Public Theology of Worship and Evangelism* (Minneapolis: Augsburg Fortress, 1992), 5.

Chapter 1: The Gospel Is Offensive. Nothing Else Should Be

1. John Piper, "Hate and Tolerance: Obstacles to the Eternal Life of Muslims," *World Magazine*, October 27, 2001, 65. Adapted from John Piper, *Brothers, We Are Not Professionals: A Plea to Pastors for Radical Ministry*, rev. ed. (Nashville: B&H, 2013), xi.
2. Timothy Keller, *Center Church: Doing Balanced, Gospel-Centered Ministry in Your City* (Grand Rapids: Zondervan, 2012), 308, emphasis mine.
3. "The Lover of God's Law Filled with Peace," Spurgeon Gems, https://www.spurgeongems.org/vols34-36/chs2004.pdf (accessed July 11, 2017).

4. Mark Dever and Paul Alexander, *The Deliberate Church: Building Your Ministry on the Gospel* (Wheaton, IL: Crossway, 2005), 44.
5. For an excellent defense of why we *should* cater to consumers, pick up a copy of *First Impressions: Creating Wow Experiences in Your Church* by my friend Mark Waltz (Loveland, CO: Group, 2013).
6. Alexander Strauch, *The Hospitality Commands: Building Loving Christian Community; Building Bridges to Friends and Neighbors* (Littleton, CO: Lewis & Roth, 1993), 17.

Chapter 2: The Sermon Starts in the Parking Lot

1. Ed Ainsworth, *Los Angeles Times*, June 23, 1955.
2. Nathan Abrams and Julie Hughes, *Containing America: Cultural Production and Consumption in 50s America* (Birmingham, UK: University of Birmingham Press, 2000), 29.
3. Horton Davies, *The Worship of the English Puritans* (Morgan, PA: Soli Deo Gloria, 1997), 182.
4. Theodore Kinni, *Be Our Guest: Perfecting the Art of Customer Service* (New York: Disney Editions, 2011), 102.

Chapter 3: When Hospitality Meets Hostility

1. Exodus 22:21; 23:9; Leviticus 19:10; 23:22; Deuteronomy 10:18–19; 24:17–21; Jeremiah 7:6; Zechariah 7:10; Malachi 3:5; et al.
2. Matthew 9:10; 15:32; Mark 2:17; Luke 7:34; 19:7, 10; and on and on.
3. Romans 12:10, 13; Hebrews 13:2; 1 Peter 4:9—you get the point.
4. J. D. Greear, *Gospel: Recovering the Power That Made Christianity Revolutionary* (Nashville: B&H, 2011), 99. (Also, I think I just proved my point about gospel-centered everything. Gospel-centered book title, anyone?)
5. Jim Henderson and Matt Casper, *Jim and Casper Go to Church: Frank Conversation about Faith, Churches, and Well-Meaning Christians* (Carol Stream, IL: Tyndale, 2007), 129.
6. Tony Evans, *Oneness Embraced: A Fresh Look at Reconciliation, the Kingdom, and Justice* (Chicago: Moody, 2011), 216.
7. John Newton, *Select Letters of John Newton* (Edinburgh: Banner of Truth Trust, 2011), 188.
8. Henderson and Casper, *Jim and Casper Go to Church*, 35.

9. Many of the points from Acts 17 come from a sermon by J. D. Greear on June 22, 2014, "Starting Where People Are." A blog version of that message can be found at https://jdgreear.com/blog/how-to-engage-nonbelievers-5-insights/.

10. Danny Meyer, *Setting the Table: The Transforming Power of Hospitality in Business* (New York: HarperCollins, 2006), 222.

Chapter 4: Beyond Parking Shuttles and Smoke Machines

1. See Tony Morgan, *Killing Cockroaches: And Other Scattered Musings on Leadership* (Nashville: B&H, 2009).

2. Timothy Keller, *Center Church: Doing Balanced, Gospel-Centered Ministry in Your City* (Grand Rapids: Zondervan, 2012), 293.

3. I owe this saying to Larry Osborne, pastor of North Coast Church in Vista, California.

4. This is not to say that I'm a proponent of "anything goes" when it comes to local church ministry, corporate worship style, or otherwise. I don't think edification happens when we head to the altar and take the rattlesnakes out of the box to prove our faith (if anything, you're proving how fast this particular middle-aged white dude can make a path and head for the door). If you want further study on fun topics like the regulative principle versus the normative principle, see chapters 6 and 7 of Mark Dever and Paul Alexander, *The Deliberate Church: Building Your Ministry on the Gospel* (Wheaton, IL: Crossway, 2005).

5. Simon Sinek, *Start with Why: How Great Leaders Inspire Everyone to Take Action* (New York: Penguin, 2009), 166–67.

6. Steve Timmis, Twitter post, September 29, 2014, 9:00 a.m., http://twitter.com/stimmis.

7. Thom Rainer, *Effective Evangelistic Churches: Successful Churches Reveal What Works and What Doesn't* (Nashville: Broadman and Holman, 1996), 169.

8. Andy Stanley and Ed Young, *Can We Do That? 24 Innovative Practices That Will Change the Way You Do Church* (West Monroe, LA: Howard, 2002), 2–3.

9. See chapter 5: "Missional or Attractional? Yes," in J. D. Greear, *Gaining by Losing: Why the Future Belongs to Churches That Send* (Grand Rapids: Zondervan, 2015), 88. Incidentally, this chapter is—in my

opinion—one of the best balances I've read of "Come and see" versus "Go and tell." We'll come back to this idea later in the book.

10. This version is adapted from Wayne Rice, *Hot Illustrations for Youth Talks: 100 Attention-Getting Stories, Parables, and Anecdotes* (El Cajon, CA: Youth Specialties, 1994), 140–42.

Chapter 5: When the Older Brother Rears His Head

1. J. D. Greear, *Gaining by Losing: Why the Future Belongs to Churches That Send* (Grand Rapids: Zondervan, 2015).

2. Andy Stanley, *Deep and Wide: Creating Churches Unchurched People Love to Attend* (Grand Rapids: Zondervan, 2012), 214.

3. I'm indebted to Ashley Wooldridge for this great line from his message "Love Does," sermon, Christ's Church of the Valley, Peoria, AZ, March 7, 2015.

4. Jerry Bridges, *The Discipline of Grace: God's Role and Our Role in the Pursuit of Holiness* (Colorado Springs: NavPress, 1994, 2006), 59–60.

5. Another great line pulled from Ashley Wooldridge, "Love Does."

Chapter 6: It's Not about You

1. This is by no means intended to be an exhaustive list of the instances of grace in the Bible. Rather, I've chosen to focus on specific instances in which God chooses to use his creation as a conduit for grace. For the exhaustive "grace list," the Bible is a great start (you should definitely read it). However, for a fantastic summation of the role of atonement and redemption in Genesis through Revelation, I have found W. A. Criswell's 1961 sermon "The Scarlet Thread through the Bible" to be the preeminent resource on the topic. More recently the Gospel Project has transcribed his sermon into a free ebook. Find it at www.gospelproject.com/criswell.

2. See the story of the Canaanite woman in Matthew 15:21–28 and Jesus's "other sheep" discourse in John 10:16. Even the parable of the wedding feast (Matthew 22:1–14) is seen by some as a precursor of the gospel spreading to Gentiles.